轻松搞定中国菜

CHINESE FOOD
MADE EASY

轻松搞定中国菜

CHINESE FOOD MADE EASY

ROSS DOBSON

murdoch books

Sydney | London

CONTENTS:

INTRODUCTION

Some say that silence in a Chinese kitchen is not a good omen. The Chinese kitchen is a place of sound and movement, of metal on metal, a cacophonous symphony producing food of pure harmony and balance.

—

In Australia, every town has a Chinese restaurant where, generally speaking, an homogenised version of Cantonese food is on offer. Canton is the former name of Guangzhou, the capital city of Guangdong Province. This region covers Hong Kong and part of mainland China. Guangzhou, Anhui, Fujian, Hunan, Jiangsu, Shandong, Szechuan and Zhejiang make up the eight culinary regions of China.

Like a tapestry, the cuisine of each region can be linked by the common thread of an ingredient or two. Yet, each region will have a distinctive and unique combination of ingredients and cooking techniques. Some differences are subtle. Some, not so.

In the cold, landlocked regions of the north, lamb and wheat-based noodles and breads dominate. Further west, the spices we associate with Indian and Middle Eastern cooking, such as cumin and dried chilli, are used to flavour lamb and beef. Meat is simply spiced and skewered, shish kebab style, then grilled or barbecued.

From the south central region of Hunan, the birthplace of Chairman Mao, comes the sweet and unctuous technique of red braising; fragrant with star anise, cinnamon quills and dark soy sauce to impart a deep caramel colour. Red-braised pork belly, sometimes called Chairman Mao's pork, has folklore status. The dish is credited with Mao's political success.

In the north-east, the food is referred to as Imperial Court cuisine. This is the home of Peking roast duck, delicately sliced so each sliver will have the perfect balance of skin, fat and meat. The slices are wrapped in wafer-thin pancakes with crisp cucumber and spring onions. The green spring onion ends are shredded and soaked in water so that they curl up like a brush. The intent is just that – they are used as a brush to apply the accompanying barbecue sauce to the pancake, before being wrapped in the pancake and eaten. This is an edible example of form following function. Very little goes to waste in the Chinese kitchen.

Szechuan, synonymous with the pepper, is a cuisine defined by a flavour called *ma la*, meaning numbing and hot. The tingling numbness comes from Szechuan pepper and the heat from prolific use of dried chillies. Sesame, seeds and oil, also makes its presence felt in the food from this region.

The provinces of the east coast use these well-known ingredients: black beans, hoi sin and plum sauces. Fresh ginger, garlic and spring onions are the celestial trinity of seasonings that kick-start a stir-fry in hot woks wrapped in flames. Here, the cacophonous clang of metal on metal is considered an essential part of good cooking.

The food from the regions of China are not only linked by ingredients and technique. Regardless of where you are, dishes all over China are often given seemingly incongruous names. 'Ants climbing tree' or 'lion's head meatballs' are intriguing names for dishes that are delicious nonetheless. Food in China is sometimes elevated to heavenly status. The symbolism is as much part of the food tradition as anything else.

THE 8 CULINARY TREASURES OF CHINA

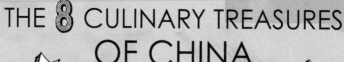

1 GUANGDONG & HONG KONG

Due to the large number of emigrants from this region, this is the style of food that many people think of as quintessentially Chinese. Most of us will know it as Cantonese. Simple steamed rice replaces wheat noodles or bread and is consumed in abundance. Steamed whole fish with ginger and spring onions, hot fresh vegetable stir-fries, bamboo baskets filled with steamed dumplings, noodle soups with barbecue pork and roasted meats.

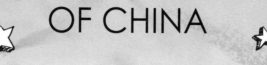

2 FUJIAN

This is a relatively small region on the coast. Seafood is dominant and much of the food is presented in a soup form. Exotic ingredients such as sharks fin, sea cucumber and dried scallops are included in Fujian dishes. A popular dish called 'Buddha jumps over the wall' is supposedly so delicious that Buddha himself would jump a wall to get to eat it.

3 ZHEJIANG

It is said that this is the most refined of China's cuisines. Fresh seafood and meat are lightly flavoured with vinegar and soy sauce. You will be hard-pressed to find any spice or chilli in the dishes of this region. Slow-simmered, perfectly cubed pieces of pork in a rich broth is known as dongpo pork and reflects the finery of this cuisine. This region is also the home of baked chicken known as 'beggars chicken' or clay-wrapped chicken.

4 JIANGSU

The wealth of the Shanghai economy makes this region one of the most affluent in China. With access to the coast and rivers, seafood is a common and popular ingredient. The best known dish to hail from this region must be classic, or Yangzhou, fried rice. A combination of chopped ham or sausage, spring onions and eggs are quickly stir-fried with rice, soy sauce and sesame oil.

⑤ SHANDONG

The birthplace of Confucius, this culinary region is on the north-east coast of China. Hearty food is popular here, such as wheat dough dumplings. These are not small delicate dumplings, but can be the size of a small hand and are filled with richly flavoured pork. Vinegar and ginger dipping sauces are served alongside the dumplings.

⑥ ANHUI

The food here is often described as hearty mountain peasant food. This landlocked region is bordered by the other more famous food regions of China and takes its culinary cue from the influences of Shandong, Jiangsu and Zhejiang. Braising, stewing and smoking are popular cooking techniques. Anhui is home to a delicious dish called Fuliji poached chicken – chicken coated in sweet syrup and flash fried in oil, then simmered in a rich stock.

⑦ HUNAN

Also known as Xiang cuisine, the food here is a reflection of the rich diversity and abundance of agriculture and produce of this region. Garlic, ginger and chilli are used with a heavy hand and give this cuisine its reputation for dry and hot food, known as *la*. A signature dish is called farmer pepper pork – tender pork belly stir-fried with green capsicums and fermented black beans.

⑧ SZECHUAN

Dishes here are defined by Szechuan peppercorns and dried red chillies. This spicy and numbing heat is known as *ma* and is the opposite of *la*. Garlic is used in abundance and many dishes are vegetarian to cater for the large number of Buddhists in this region. A good Szechuan dish has a balance of sour, pungent, hot, sweet, bitter, sour and salty flavours. This cuisine produces some of the most popular Chinese dishes, such as 'Ants climbing tree'.

INGREDIENTS FOR CHINESE COOKING

FRESH

1/ CHINESE GREENS

This covers a variety of greens: Chinese or napa cabbage, bok choy, choy sum, water spinach, snow pea shoots, to name a few. Most of these are too bitter to eat raw and cooking them brings out the sweetness. All Chinese greens are highly nutritious.

2/ CORIANDER

This uniquely flavoured and aromatic herb is used commonly, but sparingly, in Chinese cooking. Flavour is lost with long cooking times so it is added to fillings for quick-cooked dumplings or scattered over cooked meats and vegetables.

3/ GINGER

With garlic and spring onions, ginger is part of the celestial trio in Chinese cooking. It provides flavour and zesty bite to dishes. Fresh young ginger has shades of pink and yellow and is used in dipping sauces and quick stir-fries. More mature ginger is almost jade green and used in slow-cooked dishes.

4/ GARLIC

Crushed, chopped, smashed or grated, garlic is an essential fresh ingredient in Chinese cooking. Use fresh garlic with purplish, paper-like skin. Avoid ready peeled garlic, as it has far less flavour and freshness.

5/ SPRING ONIONS

This is a very mild member of the onion family and an essential fresh ingredient in Chinese cooking. Closer to the roots, the white parts are stronger in flavour and are generally cooked before eating. The vibrant green tops give crunch and flavour, sprinkled over cooked foods as a garnish.

6/ TOFU

Also known as *doufu* in Chinese, this protein-rich food has been around for millennia. It is smooth and bland and easily takes on the other flavours it is cooked with. It comes in a firm variety, which is perfect for stir-fries. Soft or silken tofu is used in soups. Both varieties can be deep fried. Tofu is a fresh ingredient and should be stored in the refrigerator. Once opened, tofu will keep in the fridge for 3–4 days.

7/ SHIITAKE MUSHROOMS

Fresh shiitake mushrooms add a rich, umami flavour to any dish. Unlike dried shiitake, which need a good soaking to render them edible, fresh shiitake are velvety soft and can be eaten raw. They need very little cooking time which makes them the perfect stir-fry ingredient.

8/ BEAN SPROUTS

Mung bean sprouts, or simply bean sprouts, are crisp and yellow and provide colour and texture to stir-fries, fried rice and fillings for spring rolls.

LIQUIDS

1/ RICE WINE

The best rice wine for cooking is from Shaoxing. Chinese cooking wine is not suitable for drinking. A combination of fermented glutinous rice, yeast and water, this wine is splashed into woks, unifying all the other flavours and seasonings. It deglazes a wok in the same way that wine is used in French cookery. It is salty, sweet and nutty and an essential ingredient in marinades for meat and slow braises.

2/ SESAME OIL

This toffee-coloured oil is made from ground toasted sesame seeds and has a distinctive warm and nutty smell. In northern China it is added to other oils in deep-frying. Sesame oil is mostly used in small amounts in stir-fries, marinades and drizzled on hot soups. With soy sauce, it is one of the essential liquid ingredients in a Chinese kitchen.

3/ OYSTER SAUCE

Oyster sauce is a common ingredient in Cantonese recipes. Despite its name, oyster sauce does not smell fishy. It imparts a sweet and gentle savoury note to stir-fries. It is really worth paying a bit more for a good-quality brand – you will definitely notice the difference. Once opened, keep it in the fridge.

4/ SOY SAUCE (DARK)

This soy sauce is very dark, rich and caramel coloured and more syrupy than light soy sauce. Although they are both called soy sauce, it is like comparing chalk and cheese. Simply put, dark soy is used in small amounts to impart colour and sweetness to slow-cooked stews.

5/ HOI SIN SAUCE

This rich, dark plum-coloured sauce is made from soy beans, vinegar, sugar and spices. It is so distinctive that you won't need to use any other sauces, except maybe some light soy sauce for extra saltiness. Its sweetness makes it perfect to use wrapped in pancakes with roasted duck, pork and lamb.

6/ SOY SAUCE (LIGHT)

Light soy sauce is saltier and thinner than dark soy. A good-quality light soy sauce will have an enticing yeasty aroma. It has a salty umami flavour that is essential to stir-fries, and it is a good table sauce to splash into soups. I believe it is preferable to dark soy as a dipping sauce, making it essential at any *yum cha* (dim sum) table.

① ② ③

④ ⑤ ⑥

⑧

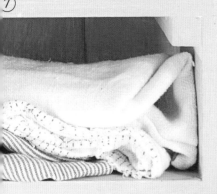

PANTRY

1/ JASMINE TEA

A fragrant and floral tea enjoyed with any meal of the day. Tea (*cha*) is also an integral part of *yum cha* (dim sum).

2/ BAMBOO SHOOTS

Canned bamboo shoots are the sweet, young tender shoots of a particular variety of bamboo that provide colour, sweetness and crunch to stir-fries. They come finely shredded or julienned.

3/ DRIED SHRIMP

Bags of very small, pungent dried shrimp can be found at Asian food stores, but the better-quality dried shrimp is kept in the refrigerator. These can be pounded and added to stir-fries.

4/ BEAN THREAD NOODLES

These mung bean noodles are more versatile than wheat-based noodles as they hold their shape and won't absorb the liquid they are cooked in. They are also gluten free.

5/ WATER CHESTNUTS

Grown in the watery environment of a rice paddy, water chestnuts conveniently come in a tin and are ready to use. They add crunch and freshness to dumpling fillings and stir-fries.

6/ SHIITAKE MUSHROOMS

Dried shiitake mushrooms need a good soaking in boiling water prior to use in stir-fries or in a filling for dumplings. Cooked and canned shiitake mushrooms also make a convenient addition to soups and stir-fries.

7/ PRESERVED BLACK BEANS

These are soy beans that have been fermented with salt and spices. They have a rich and funky aroma and add umami flavour to stir-fries. Give them a good rinse before use to remove excess salt, and roughly mash. You can find these in specialty Asian stores.

8/ CORNFLOUR

Cornflour can be used to thicken soups, stews and stir-fries, or added to a marinade to help it cling to the meat. Used with plain flour in a batter, it gives a crisp, crunchy coating to fried foods.

CHINESE MUST-HAVE SPICES

1/ CHILLI POWDER

Chilli powder (finely ground dried chillies) is used sparingly in Chinese cookery. This spice is combined with other spices such as salt, five-spice powder and all the varieties of pepper and sprinkled over fried foods.

2/ CASSIA BARK

These curled pieces of wood are shavings from the bark of the cinnamon tree, and are a fragrant addition to slow-cooked stews and braises. Chinese cinnamon sticks look less refined and more organic than other cinnamon. They are added whole to liquid ingredients and slowly impart their sweet flavour to braised chicken, beef or pork. This spice is one of the essential flavours in what is called 'red braising'.

3/ DRIED CHILLI

The source of heat in many Szechuan dishes, dried chillies are often used whole and in abundance. They are the source of the spicy heat (*la*) and Szechuan pepper is the numbing heat effect (*ma*) in Szechuan dishes. Dried chillies are added whole to stir-fries where they impart a smokiness.

4/ FIVE-SPICE POWDER

The quintessential Chinese spice that is actually a combination of other spices, which generally include cardamom, cinnamon, cloves, fennel seeds and Szechuan peppercorns. In combination with salt, this spice is rubbed over the skin of meat before being fried and roasted.

5/ SZECHUAN PEPPERCORNS

Despite the name, these are not a pepper but a berry from the prickly ash tree. They are very common in Szechuan dishes and provide the numbness or tingling sensation known as the *ma* as opposed to the *la*, which is the fiery heat from dried chillies.

6/ STAR ANISE

The visual beauty of this spice is matched only by its potent and intoxicating aroma. It is similar to anise seed but much more robust. Star anise is an essential flavour component of Chinese five-spice.

7/ WHITE PEPPER

White pepper is much more common in Chinese cooking than black pepper. While it is less intense and aromatic than black pepper, white pepper is more floral and sweet and provides a gentle spicy heat. White pepper really enhances the flavour of soups and stir-fries.

8/ SALT

The best salt to use in Chinese cooking is fine sea salt (sometimes known as kosher salt). Table salt is more one-dimensional and can overpower anything it is added to. Sea salt is less 'salty', with a more complex flavour that complements foods.

STARTERS & SOUPS

前菜和湯

SPRING ONION PANCAKES

葱油餅

MAKES: 4   PREPARATION: 20 MINUTES   RESTING: 30 MINUTES   COOKING: 6 MINUTES

FRESH

175 ml boiling water

65 g finely sliced spring onions

PANTRY

300 g plain flour, plus extra for
  dusting

½ teaspoon baking powder

½ teaspoon fine sea salt

1 tablespoon sesame oil

125 ml vegetable oil

These rustic looking snacks are very moreish. Lightly pan-fried until crisp, they can be served as part of a banquet or are delicious as a starter accompanied by chilli sauce and a cold beer.

—

Combine the flour, baking powder and salt in a food processor. With the motor running, add the boiling water and process until the mixture forms into a ball. If needed, add 1 or 2 extra tablespoons of water to bring the mixture together.

Tip the dough onto a lightly floured surface and knead for a few minutes to form a smooth disc shape. Cover in plastic wrap and set aside for 30 minutes.

Combine the sesame oil and half the vegetable oil in a small bowl.

Divide the dough into 4 pieces. Working with one portion at a time, roll out on a lightly floured surface to a very thin 20 cm circle. Brush some of the oil mix over the dough and sprinkle over one-quarter of the spring onions.

Starting at the end nearest you, roll the pastry into a log enclosing the spring onions. Now starting from one end, firmly roll into a coil or snail shape, tucking the end in. Repeat with the remaining dough.

On a lightly floured surface, roll each coil roughly into a 20 cm circle. Put the dough on a plate with pieces of baking paper between each one and chill until needed. These can be made a day or two in advance.

To cook the pancakes, heat the remaining oil in a large non-stick frying pan over medium heat. Cook each pancake for 2–3 minutes on each side until golden and crispy. Cut into wedges or roughly tear to serve.

TEA & STAR ANISE EGGS

五香茶葉蛋

SERVES: 8 AS A SIDE   *PREPARATION:* 5 MINUTES   *STEEPING:* 6 HOURS
COOKING: 2 ¼ HOURS

FRESH

8 eggs

SPICES

1 quantity Five-spice (see page 213)

PANTRY

2 teaspoons salt

2 tablespoons dark soy sauce

2 black tea bags

These exotic-looking eggs are simple to prepare and make an impressive starter or snack. Hidden under the shell is a beautifully crazed marbled egg.

—

Put the eggs in a saucepan and add enough cold water to cover. Bring to the boil and cook for 10 minutes. Rinse under cold water until completely cold.

Use the back of a spoon to tap the egg shell so it is cracked all over. Set aside.

Put 1.5 litres cold water in a small saucepan. Add the Five-spice, salt, dark soy sauce and tea bags. Bring to the boil, then reduce the heat to a low simmer.

Add the eggs and cook for 2 hours, adjusting the heat to maintain a low simmer.

Remove from the heat, leaving the eggs in the liquid. Transfer to the fridge and leave to steep for 6 hours. Peel and serve.

SIU MAI
(PORK & PRAWN DUMPLINGS)

燒賣（豬肉、蝦肉餡）

SERVES: 4   *PREPARATION:* 10 MINUTES   *RESTING:* 30 MINUTES   *CHILLING:* 3-6 HOURS
COOKING: 15 MINUTES

FRESH

250 g minced pork

50 g raw prawns, roughly chopped

2 teaspoons finely grated ginger

12 wonton wrappers

Chilli Sauce (see page 210), to serve

PANTRY

2 dried shiitake mushrooms

2 teaspoons light soy sauce

2 teaspoons cornflour

Yum cha **(dim sum) is usually served between 10 am and
3 pm. Small morsels are enjoyed with tea. But it is also a very
social occasion, as the food and tea act as a backdrop to family
gatherings and business meetings.**

—

Put the mushrooms in a small heatproof bowl. Pour over boiling
water to cover. Leave for 30 minutes, or until the caps are soft.
Drain well, then remove and discard the stems. Finely chop the caps
and put into a bowl.

Add the pork, prawns, ginger, soy sauce and cornflour to the
mushrooms. Use your hands to mix everything together so it is
evenly combined. Cover and refrigerate for 3–6 hours for the flavours
to develop.

To make the dumplings, place a wrapper in the palm of your hand.
Put a heaped tablespoon of the filling in the centre of the wrapper.
Fold up the edges to wrap around the filling, leaving the top of the
dumpling uncovered. Firmly wrap your thumb and index finger
around the top of the dumpling so it resembles a little bag.

Sit the dumplings in a bamboo steamer lined with baking paper. Place
the steamer over a pan of simmering water and steam for 15 minutes
until the dumplings are cooked through. Serve hot from the steamer
or transfer to a small plate and serve with Chilli Sauce and some soy
sauce and sesame seeds on the side.

STEAMED PRAWN & RICE NOODLE ROLLS

春卷的做法

SERVES: 4 *PREPARATION: 15 MINUTES* *COOKING: 10 MINUTES*

FRESH

16 frozen raw prawns, peeled and deveined

1 quantity Chilli & Soy Sauce (see page 214)

4 rice noodle sheets

8 snow peas (mangetout) – half sliced

PANTRY

½ teaspoon light soy sauce

½ teaspoon Chinese rice wine

You will find a variety of rice noodles in Asian specialty stores: round ones like thick spaghetti to use in soups; flat rice noodles for stir-fries; and sheets of rice noodles that, when unravelled, resemble white sheets of pasta. Store them at room temperature – chilling them will cause the noodles to turn brittle and crack.

—

Defrost the prawns and pat dry with a paper towel. Put the prawns in a bowl with the Chilli and Soy Sauce, light soy sauce and rice wine. Toss the prawns around in the mixture. Set aside for 15 minutes.

Unroll the rice noodle sheets. Cut them into 20 cm squares and lay them on a clean work surface.

Put 4 prawns along the length closest to you, about 2 cm from the edge. Roll the noodle to firmly enclose the prawns and transfer to a heatproof plate that will fit inside a steamer basket. Repeat to make 4 rolls, then sit the plate in the steamer basket.

Bring a saucepan of water to the boil. Sit the basket on top, cover and steam for 10 minutes until the prawns are cooked through and the rice noodles are soft. Serve hot with the snow peas and more Chilli and Soy Sauce on the side.

PORK & CABBAGE
SPRING ROLLS

卷心菜豬肉卷

MAKES: 6   PREPARATION: 20 MINUTES   COOKING: 20 MINUTES

FRESH

300 g minced pork

2 teaspoons finely grated ginger

1 carrot, coarsely grated

300 g finely shredded Chinese cabbage

SPICE

1 teaspoon Five-spice Salt
   (see page 213)

PANTRY

2 tablespoons oyster sauce

6 spring roll wrappers

1 teaspoon cornflour

vegetable oil, for frying

plum sauce, to serve

Spring rolls are a really tasty starter. They can be made in advance, kept in the fridge and cooked to order. It won't take long to master rolling them and they freeze really well, too.

—

Combine the minced pork and 1 tablespoon of the oyster sauce. Mix the remaining oyster sauce and 2 tablespoons cold water in a small bowl or jug and set aside.

Heat 1 tablespoon vegetable oil in a wok over high heat. Add the ginger, carrot and cabbage and stir-fry for 2 minutes until the vegetables are tender.

Add the pork mixture and sprinkle over the Five-spice Salt. Stir-fry for 2 minutes until the pork is no longer pink. Stir through the diluted oyster sauce. Cook for 1 minute until the sauce thickens, then transfer to a bowl and leave to cool.

To roll the spring rolls, take a wrapper and place on a clean surface with a corner facing you. Combine the cornflour and 1 tablespoon cold water in a small bowl.

Put 3 tablespoons of the pork mixture on the corner near you and brush around the edge of the wrapper with the cornflour mixture. Roll into a cigar shape, folding in the sides as you go. Repeat to make 6 spring rolls.

To cook the spring rolls, add enough oil to come one-third up the side of a wok. Heat over medium–high heat. The oil is ready if a cube of bread turns golden in 10–15 seconds. Add 4 spring rolls and cook for 3–4 minutes until golden and crispy. Transfer to a plate lined with paper towel to absorb any excess oil. Repeat to cook the remaining spring rolls. Serve hot with plum sauce on the side.

PRAWN SPRING ROLLS

鮮蝦春卷

MAKES: 6   PREPARATION: 10 MINUTES   RESTING: 15 MINUTES
COOKING: 10 MINUTES

FRESH

250 g peeled and deveined raw prawns
   (about 18)

1 tablespoon finely grated ginger

30 g finely chopped garlic chives

Chilli Sauce (see page 210), to serve

PANTRY

1 teaspoon light soy sauce

6 egg-free spring roll wrappers

75 g sesame seeds

vegetable oil, for frying

Ready-made spring roll wrappers can be bought with or without egg. The white, eggless ones are what you need here. These pretty looking rolls are encrusted with sesame seeds on one side.

—

Combine the prawns, ginger, garlic chives and soy sauce in a bowl. Set aside for 15 minutes.

To roll the spring rolls, take a wrapper and place on a clean surface with a corner facing you. Lay 3 tablespoons of the prawn mixture in a row on the corner nearest you. Brush around the edge of the wrapper with cold water. Roll the pointed edge of the wrapper up and over the filling, fold in the two sides and firmly roll. Repeat to make 6 spring rolls.

Put the sesame seeds on a plate. Lightly brush the smooth side of the spring roll with water. Dip into the sesame seeds to coat.

To cook the spring rolls, add enough oil to come one-third up the side of a wok. Heat over medium–high heat. The oil is ready if a cube of bread turns golden in 10–15 seconds. Add half the spring rolls and cook for 2–3 minutes until the sesame seeds are golden. Transfer to a plate lined with paper towel to absorb any excess oil. Repeat to cook the remaining spring rolls. Serve with Chilli Sauce on the side.

BEAN CURD SPRING ROLLS

黃金腐皮卷

SERVES: 8 AS A STARTER   *PREPARATION: 30 MINUTES*   *COOKING: 15 MINUTES*

FRESH

1 carrot, coarsely grated

1 celery stick, finely sliced

150 g finely sliced Chinese cabbage

4 fresh shiitake mushrooms, finely sliced

2 spring onions, finely sliced

Chilli & Soy Sauce (see page 214), to serve

PANTRY

vegetable oil, for frying

3 teaspoons plain flour

1 teaspoon light soy sauce

4 bean curd skins

These vegan spring rolls are made from bean curd sheets (or skins). You need to look for soft sheets and the best way to test for this is to bend them in the packet. They should not break or crack when bent. One packet will have more than four sheets but they can be stored in an airtight bag for later use.

—

Heat the vegetable oil in a wok over high heat. Swirl the wok around so that it is coated in oil. Add the carrot, celery, cabbage, mushrooms and spring onions and stir-fry for 3–4 minutes until all the vegetables are tender.

Sprinkle 2 teaspoons of the flour over the vegetables and stir-fry to combine. Add the soy sauce and 3 tablespoons water and stir-fry for 1 minute until the mixture has thickened. Transfer to a bowl and leave to cool.

Cut 4 squares from the bean curd, each measuring about 30 cm. Lay them on a clean work surface and wipe with a damp cloth to soften them slightly.

Combine the remaining flour with 2 teaspoons cold water in a bowl. Brush around the edges of the bean curd.

Put one-quarter of the filling in the centre of each bean curd square. Fold the edge nearest you up and over the filling, fold the sides in, then roll up into a log shape.

Add enough oil to come one-third up the side of a wok and heat over medium–high heat. The oil is ready when a cube of bread turns golden brown in 10–15 seconds. Add the rolls and cook for 5 minutes, turning them so they cook to an even golden colour. Transfer to a plate lined with paper towel. Serve with the Chilli and Soy Sauce.

DUMPLINGS TWO WAYS
餃子的兩種做法

SERVES: 4   *PREPARATION: 20 MINUTES*   *RESTING: 1 HOUR*   *COOKING: 10 MINUTES*

FRESH

150 g finely chopped Chinese cabbage

300 g minced pork

1 tablespoon finely grated ginger

1 quantity Dumpling Dough
  (see page 218) or ready-made
  dumpling wrappers

Szechuan Dipping Sauce
  (see page 214), to serve

PANTRY

2 teaspoons fine sea salt

1 teaspoon light soy sauce

1 tablespoon vegetable oil

It's more common in northern China for dumplings to be boiled. They can also be pan-fried and are known as 'potstickers'. They develop a crusty, golden base before being steamed in the pan.

—

Combine the cabbage and salt in a colander and massage in the salt. Set the colander over a bowl. Leave for 30 minutes, so excess liquid drains from the cabbage. Squeeze the cabbage firmly to remove as much excess liquid as possible. Discard the liquid.

Put the cabbage in a bowl with the pork, ginger and soy sauce. Stir until well combined. Cover and set aside for 30 minutes.

To make the dumplings, put 2 teaspoons of the pork mixture in the centre of 1 circle of dumpling dough. Wet the edges of the dough with water and fold over the edges to seal together. Crimp or pleat the edges and gently tap them on a work surface to flatten the base. Repeat to make 24 dumplings.

To boil the dumplings: cook in boiling water for 8–10 minutes until they rise to the top. Drain well and transfer to a serving plate.

To pan-fry the dumplings: heat the vegetable oil in a large frying pan over medium–high heat, swirling the pan around to coat in the oil. Add the dumplings to the pan and cook for 2–3 minutes, so the bases of the dough develop a golden crust. Add 240 ml boiling water to the pan and shake the pan to remove any stuck bits. Cover the pan and cook for 5–6 minutes, until the dumplings are cooked through and the water has evaporated.

Serve with Szechuan Dipping Sauce.

STEAMED PRAWN DUMPLINGS WITH SZECHUAN CHILLI SAUCE

四川辣醬配蝦餃

SERVES: 4   **PREPARATION:** 10 MINUTES   **RESTING:** 15 MINUTES   **COOKING:** 5 MINUTES

FRESH

150 g raw peeled prawns, chopped

1 teaspoon finely grated ginger

15 g roughly chopped coriander

16 square egg wonton wrappers

PANTRY

½ teaspoon light soy sauce

1 teaspoon cornflour

Szechuan Dipping Sauce
  (see page 214), to serve

These prawn-filled dumplings look so pretty and silky on the plate they are almost too good to eat. They can be served floating on Szechuan dipping sauce.

—

Combine the prawns, ginger, 1 tablespoon of the coriander and the soy sauce in a food processor. Process for a few seconds until the mixture is finely chopped. Transfer to a bowl, cover and set aside for 15 minutes for the flavours to develop.

Put 2 teaspoons of the prawn mixture in the centre of each wonton wrapper. Brush the edges with cold water and fold the opposite points of the wrapper together to form a triangle. Press the edges together to enclose the filling. Wet the opposite points of the triangle with water and press together to seal, forming a dumpling that resembles tortellini. Set aside.

Bring a saucepan of water to the boil and cook the dumplings for 5 minutes until they rise to the top and are cooked through. Drain well and transfer to a serving plate. Pour over the Szechuan Dipping Sauce and scatter with the remaining coriander.

CHICKEN NOODLE SOUP

鶏肉蛋面

SERVES: 4   *PREPARATION: 22 MINUTES*   *COOKING: 1¼ HOURS*

FRESH

3 spring onions, cut into 10 cm
    lengths, plus extra slices to serve

10 cm piece fresh ginger, sliced

bunch coriander

2 chicken breast fillets

400 g thin egg noodles

PANTRY

2 tablespoons light soy sauce,
    plus extra to serve

sesame oil, to drizzle

It seems that every cuisine has its own version of chicken soup. A very simple stock recipe is given here. To make a cheat's version of this, use a good-quality ready-made stock and a shredded shop-bought rotisserie chicken, but poaching the chicken yourself is very easy and makes for delicious stock.

—

Put the spring onions, ginger, the coriander roots and stems (reserving the leaves) and the soy sauce in a saucepan with 2 litres cold water. Bring to the boil over high heat. When the stock boils, add the chicken. Cover the pan with a lid and remove from the heat. Leave the chicken to poach in the stock for 1 hour.

Use a slotted spoon to transfer the chicken to a chopping board. Strain the stock and return to a clean saucepan. Discard the ingredients in the sieve.

Use your fingers to roughly shred the meat and transfer it to the stock. Cook over low heat while cooking the noodles.

Bring another saucepan of water to the boil. Add the noodles and cook for 2–3 minutes until just tender. Drain well and transfer to 4 large serving bowls.

Ladle the soup over the noodles. Serve scattered with the spring onion slices and reserved coriander leaves. Drizzle with sesame oil and the extra soy sauce to taste.

HOT & SOUR SOUP

酸辣濃湯

SERVES: 8 AS A SIDE   PREPARATION: 5 MINUTES   COOKING: 10 MINUTES

FRESH

2 tomatoes, cut into bite-sized pieces

200 g fresh shiitake mushrooms (about 8–10), diced

300 g silken tofu, cut into 2 cm pieces

25 g roughly chopped coriander

SPICE

½ teaspoon ground white pepper

PANTRY

50 g sliced bamboo shoots

1.5 litres chicken stock

3 tablespoons black vinegar

1 tablespoon cornflour

The combination of fresh tomatoes, vinegar and pepper makes this soup taste light, spicy and tangy all at once! A small bowl of this will really get the taste buds going and would be a perfect soup to serve as part of a banquet.

—

Combine the bamboo shoots, stock and vinegar in a saucepan over high heat. Bring to the boil, then add the tomatoes and mushrooms. Cook for 5 minutes until the mushrooms are cooked through.

Add the white pepper, tofu and half the coriander.

Combine the cornflour with 2 tablespoons cold water to make a paste. Stir into the soup and boil for 2 minutes until the soup thickens.

Transfer to serving bowls with the remaining coriander scattered over the soup.

SAN CHOY BOW
(STIR-FRIED PORK IN LETTUCE CUPS)

生菜包

SERVES: 4   *PREPARATION: 10 MINUTES*   *CHILLING: 3-6 HOURS*   *COOKING: 10 MINUTES*

FRESH

300 g minced pork

90 g fresh shiitake mushrooms, sliced

1 carrot, finely grated

bunch garlic chives, cut into
   2 cm pieces

8 iceberg lettuce leaves

PANTRY

3 tablespoons oyster sauce

2 tablespoons vegetable oil

45 g coarsely chopped water
   chestnuts

The best way to remove lettuce leaves is to break off the stem of the lettuce and soak the whole head in cold water for 10 minutes. This will make it very easy to peel away perfect lettuce 'cups' that are fully intact, crisp and fresh.

—

Combine the pork with 1 tablespoon of the oyster sauce. Cover and refrigerate for 3–6 hours.

Heat 1 tablespoon of the oil in a wok over high heat. Swirl the wok around to coat in the oil. Add the mushrooms, carrots and garlic chives and stir-fry for 3–4 minutes until the carrots are just tender. Remove the vegetables to a plate.

Add the remaining oil to the wok. Swirl the wok around to coat in the oil. Add the pork and cook, without stirring, for 2 minutes, so the pork can caramelise and develop a golden crust. Stir-fry the pork for a further 2 minutes until brown.

Return all the vegetables to the wok and add the water chestnuts and remaining oyster sauce. Stir-fry for 2 minutes until hot and well combined.

Transfer to a serving plate and serve with lettuce leaves on the side to wrap up the mixture.

CHICKEN SWEETCORN SOUP

粟米羹

SERVES: 8 AS A STARTER   *PREPARATION:* 10 MINUTES   *COOKING:* 1¼ HOURS

FRESH

2 chicken breast fillets

50 g roughly chopped coriander

PANTRY

1.5 litres chicken stock

400 g tin sweetcorn, drained

400 g tin creamed corn

2 tablespoons cornflour

1 tablespoon sesame oil

Chicken and sweetcorn together make a perennial favourite. The subtle flavours are also a great introduction to Chinese cuisine for kids.

—

Put the stock in a saucepan over high heat. When the stock boils, add the chicken. Cover the pan and remove from the heat. Leave for 1 hour until the chicken is white and cooked through.

Use a slotted spoon to transfer the chicken to a chopping board and leave to cool. When cool enough to handle, cut into 1–2 cm pieces.

Return to the stock and add the corn and creamed corn. Return to high heat and bring to the boil.

Combine the cornflour with 2 tablespoons cold water to make a thin paste. Stir the paste through the boiling soup and cook for 2 minutes until the soup thickens.

Divide the soup between 8 small serving bowls. Top with coriander and a drizzle of sesame oil.

PRAWN TOASTS

蝦多士

SERVES: 4   *PREPARATION: 20 MINUTES*   *COOKING: 5 MINUTES*

FRESH

300 g raw peeled prawns

2 spring onions, finely chopped

small bunch coriander, leaves
  roughly chopped

6 slices white bread, crusts removed

PANTRY

1 teaspoon cornflour

1 teaspoon light soy sauce

75 g sesame seeds

vegetable oil, for frying

plum sauce, to serve

The sesame seeds will magically stick to the fried triangles of bread topped with prawns. Like many Chinese starters, these make ideal party or finger food. The mixture can be whipped up a day in advance.

—

Place the prawns, spring onions, coriander, cornflour and soy sauce in a food processor and blend to a chunky paste. Transfer to a bowl.

Spread the prawn mixture over one side of each slice of bread. Cut into triangles.

Put the sesame seeds in a small bowl. Press the bread triangles, prawn side down, in the sesame seeds, then transfer to a baking tray.

Fill a wok one-third full with the vegetable oil and heat over medium heat. The oil is ready if a small cube of bread sizzles on contact with the oil and browns within 10–15 seconds.

Add half the prawn breads to the oil and cook for 2 minutes, turning in the oil so they become golden. Transfer to a tray lined with paper towel. Repeat to cook the remaining toasts. Arrange on a serving plate and serve with some plum sauce for dipping.

CRISPY CHICKEN WINGS
WITH SPICED SALT

椒鹽鷄翼

SERVES: 4 **PREPARATION:** *10 MINUTES* **CHILLING:** *6 HOURS* **COOKING:** *30 MINUTES*

FRESH

8 chicken wings, wing tips
   removed (optional)

lemon wedges, to serve

SPICES

Five-spice Salt (see page 213)

PANTRY

3 tablespoons dark soy sauce

3 tablespoons light soy sauce

100 g brown sugar

vegetable oil, for frying

Fried chicken wings taste so good because they are usually marinated or brined before frying. The salt and sugar in the brining mixture is absorbed by the chicken, rendering the flesh sweet and succulent.

—

Combine 3 litres water, both soy sauces and the brown sugar in a large saucepan and bring to the boil over medium heat, then cook for 15 minutes for the flavours to develop.

Add the chicken wings, cover the pot and remove from the heat. Leave for 1 hour to cool.

Put the wings on a baking tray and refrigerate for 6 hours until they are cold and very dry.

To cook the wings, fill a wok one-third full with the vegetable oil and heat over medium heat. The oil is ready if a small cube of bread sizzles on contact with the oil and browns within 10–15 seconds.

Add 4 of the wings and fry for 5–6 minutes, turning often so they cook to a golden colour all over. Transfer to a plate lined with paper towel to absorb any excess oil. Repeat with the remaining wings.

Put the wings on a serving plate and serve with the Five-spice Salt and lemon wedges on the side.

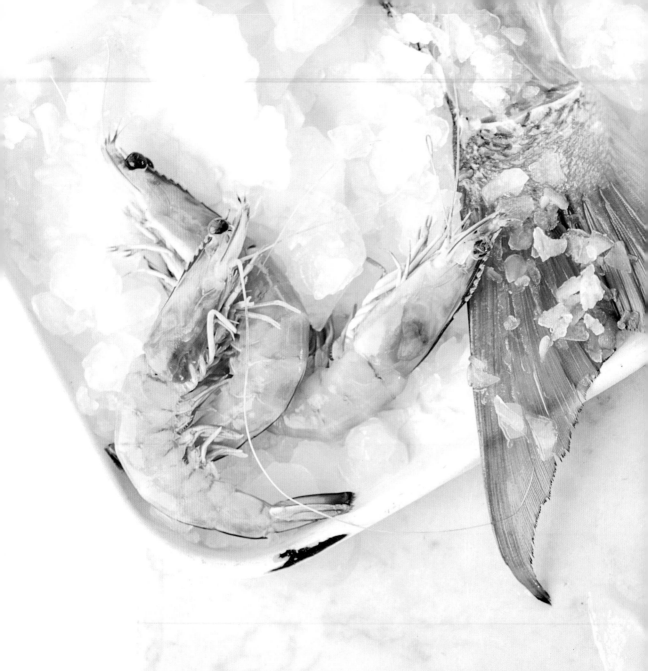

SEAFOOD

海鮮

SEAFOOD IN XO SAUCE

醬炒海鮮

SERVES: 4 TO SHARE   *PREPARATION: 10 MINUTES*   *COOKING: 10 MINUTES*

FRESH

3 cm piece fresh ginger, peeled
  and finely chopped

3 spring onions, cut into 4–5 cm lengths

1 red capsicum (pepper), seeded and
  cut into 2 cm pieces

750 g mixed seafood (white fish,
  scallops, prawns, calamari),
  chopped into bite-sized pieces

Steamed Rice (see page 215), to serve

PANTRY

1 tablespoon vegetable oil

3 tablespoons XO sauce

3 tablespoons Chinese rice wine

XO is a reference to Extra Old Brandy which is considered an affluent and exclusive product. XO sauce is made from expensive ingredients like dried scallops and shrimp. The sauce comes already full of flavour so best to keep things simple whenever you include it in a recipe. Hand-pick your own favourite seafood or, for convenience, use a good-quality frozen seafood mix.

—

Heat the vegetable oil in a wok over high heat. Swirl the wok around to coat in the oil. Add the ginger, spring onions and capsicum and stir-fry for 2 minutes.

Add the seafood and cook for 1 minute, without stirring, then gently stir-fry for 1 minute until the seafood is golden and almost cooked through.

Stir through the XO sauce until it is well combined and fragrant.

Add the rice wine to the wok, pouring it in around the sides. Cook for 1–2 minutes, so the wine has almost evaporated and the XO sauce is glossy. Serve hot with steamed rice.

SALT & PEPPER SQUID

椒鹽雙魷

SERVES: 4 TO SHARE   *PREPARATION:* 10 MINUTES   *COOKING:* 10 MINUTES

FRESH

500 g squid hoods

small handful coriander leaves,
  roughly chopped

lemon wedges, to serve

SPICES

1 quantity Chilli Salt (see page 212)

PANTRY

150 g plain flour

vegetable oil, for frying

This popular recipe can so easily be made at home with a few pantry staples. You need the whole squid hood for this recipe so they can be sliced into lengths and flash fried. They need nothing more than a dusting of flour.

—

Cut the squid hoods open. Use a sharp knife to clean the inside of the squid and then finely slice. Rinse under cold water and pat dry. Store on a flat tray in the fridge, uncovered, until ready to cook.

When ready to cook, put the flour on a plate.

Add enough oil to come one-third of the way up the sides of a wok and heat over high heat. The oil is ready when a cube of bread sizzles on contact and browns in 10–15 seconds.

Toss a handful of the squid in the flour to coat. Shake off excess flour. Gently add the squid to the oil and cook for 2–3 minutes until golden and tender. Transfer to a plate lined with paper towel. Repeat to cook the remaining squid.

Put the squid in a bowl. Add 2 teaspoons of the Chilli Salt and toss to combine.

Scatter the coriander leaves over the squid and squeeze some lemon juice over the top. Serve the extra Chilli Salt on the side.

STEAMED WHOLE FISH WITH GINGER & SPRING ONIONS

薑葱蒸魚

SERVES: *4 TO SHARE*   **PREPARATION:** *15 MINUTES*   **COOKING:** *20 MINUTES*

FRESH

1 whole fish, approximately 1.2 kg
(snapper, bream), cleaned and scaled

3 spring onions, finely sliced
into matchsticks

20 g piece fresh ginger, peeled and
finely sliced into matchsticks

handful coriander leaves and stems,
roughly chopped

Steamed Rice (see page 215), to serve

Chilli Sauce (see page 210),
to serve (optional)

PANTRY

1 tablespoon Chinese rice wine

1 tablespoon light soy sauce

3 tablespoons vegetable oil

This dish is so very typical of Cantonese cookery, where freshness is paramount. In Chinese restaurants, large tanks store live seafood which are often presented alive to customers as a guarantee of freshness.

—

Cut the fish 3–4 times on each side, ensuring the cuts go through to the bones. This will enable the fish to cook evenly.

Choose a wok or large saucepan that will snugly fit a large bamboo steamer basket on top. Half fill with water and bring to the boil. Sit the fish on a heatproof plate that will fit inside the bamboo steamer basket. Pour over the rice wine and soy sauce.

Scatter the spring onions and ginger over the fish. Sit the plate in the basket, cover and steam for 15 minutes until the flesh is white and easily removed from the bones with a fork. Remove from the heat.

Heat the vegetable oil in a small saucepan over high heat. When the oil is smoking hot, quickly and carefully pour over the top of the fish, causing the spring onions and ginger to sizzle.

Scatter the coriander over the fish and serve hot with steamed rice and fresh Chilli Sauce, if using.

STIR-FRIED MUSSELS WITH BLACK BEAN & CHILLI

豆豉炒鮮蚵

SERVES: 4 TO SHARE   *PREPARATION: 10 MINUTES*   *COOKING: 10 MINUTES*

FRESH

2 tablespoons Chilli Sauce
  (see page 210)

1 kg mussels, de-bearded and scrubbed

bunch coriander, roughly chopped

Steamed Rice (see page 215), to serve

PANTRY

1 tablespoon vegetable oil

80 ml Chinese rice wine

2 tablespoons black beans,
  roughly mashed

1 tablespoon light soy sauce

Mussels are a convenient ingredient as they are often sold ready to cook in airtight bags. Alternatively, mussels will need a light scrubbing and de-bearding prior to cooking. Here, they are cooked quickly with a classic combination of black bean and chilli.

—

Heat the oil in a wok over high heat. Add the Chilli Sauce and stir-fry for just a few seconds to flavour the oil. Add the rice wine and cook for a few seconds.

Add the black beans, soy sauce and 360 ml water and bring to the boil. Add the mussels, cover the wok and cook for about 5 minutes until the mussels start to open.

Stir through half the coriander and remove from the heat. Transfer to a large serving bowl and scatter over the remaining coriander. Serve with steamed rice.

SEAFOOD HOTPOT WITH VERMICELLI NOODLES

粉絲海鮮鍋

SERVES: 4 TO SHARE   *PREPARATION: 10 MINUTES*   *CHILLING: 30 MINUTES*
COOKING: 15 MINUTES

FRESH

500 g mixed seafood

5 cm piece fresh ginger, peeled and finely sliced

150 g roughly chopped Chinese cabbage

small bunch of coriander, roughly chopped, to serve

PANTRY

2 tablespoons light soy sauce

100 g vermicelli noodles

720 ml good-quality fish or chicken stock

This is a delicious and comforting recipe that requires very little effort. Ready-made mixed seafood comes ready to go but you can hand-pick your preferred seafood for this. You may choose to use only one type of seafood such as fish fillets, scallops or prawns.

—

Put the seafood, ginger and 1 tablespoon of the soy sauce in a bowl. Mix to combine. Cover and refrigerate for 30 minutes.

Put the noodles in a bowl and cover with warm water. Leave for 10 minutes, then drain. Tip into a bowl. Use a pair of kitchen scissors to roughly chop the noodles.

Combine the stock, cabbage and remaining soy sauce and bring to the boil over medium heat in a Chinese clay pot or casserole dish. Add the noodles.

Put the seafood and marinade on top of the noodles. Cover the pot and cook for 8–10 minutes until the seafood is cooked through.

Serve with coriander scattered over.

STEAMED PRAWNS

蒸大蝦

SERVES: 4 TO SHARE   **PREPARATION:** *20 MINUTES*   **COOKING:** *10 MINUTES*

FRESH

500 g large raw prawns

Chilli & Soy Sauce (see page 214),
  to serve

SPICES

½ teaspoon fine sea salt

PANTRY

2 tablespoons Chinese rice wine

½ teaspoon white sugar

Here sweet and fresh prawns are steamed in their shells. It makes for a truly shared treat at the table. Make sure the prawns are served with finger bowls and napkins as this gets messy!

—

Combine the prawns in a bowl with the rice wine, salt and sugar. Set aside for 15 minutes.

Line a bamboo steamer basket with baking paper. Tumble the prawns into the basket.

Sit a metal rack in a wok. Add water to the wok, ensuring the level is below that of the rack. Bring the water to the boil over high heat.

When the water boils, sit the basket on the rack. Cover and steam for 10 minutes, until the prawns are pink and cooked through. Serve directly from the basket with the Chilli and Soy Sauce on the side.

How to:
PEEL PRAWNS
如何剝蝦

While frozen peeled prawns are very convenient, there is nothing quite as good as the texture of a fresh prawn. The heads and shells can be used to make a very tasty stock.

EQUIPMENT

 kitchen paper

 small sharp knife

baking tray

1

Hold a prawn head with the thumb and first two fingers of one hand and hold the tail and lower part of the body with the opposite thumb and fingers.

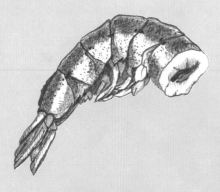

Twist the head and as you do so, pull it away from the body...

and discard.

2

Pull off

and discard all the legs on the underbelly of the prawn.

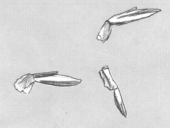

3 *Peel off* each segment of shell from the body of the prawn, starting from the head end...

and discard.

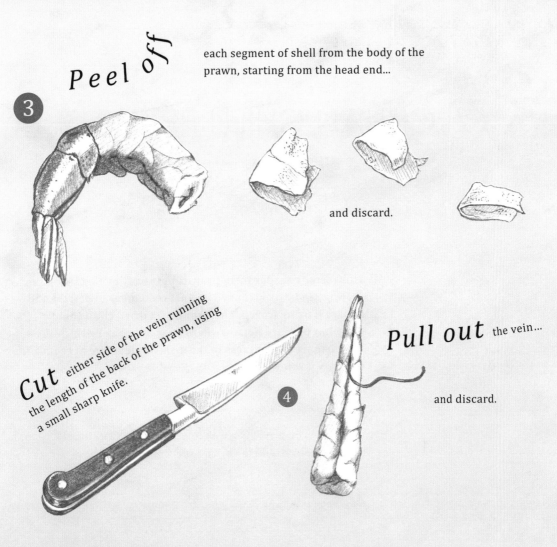

Cut either side of the vein running the length of the back of the prawn, using a small sharp knife.

4

Pull out the vein...

and discard.

Wash under cold water and...

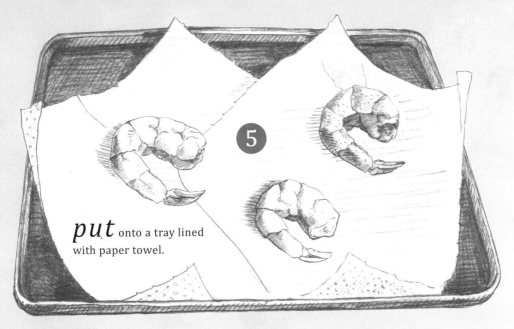

5

put onto a tray lined with paper towel.

Refrigerate until needed.

SZECHUAN CHILLI PRAWNS

四川香辣蝦

SERVES: *4 TO SHARE*   **PREPARATION:** *10 MINUTES*   **COOKING:** *5-6 MINUTES*

FRESH

2 spring onions, finely chopped

3 cm piece fresh ginger,
  finely chopped

3 garlic cloves, finely chopped

24 raw prawns, peeled and deveined

SPICE

20 g large dried chillies

PANTRY

2 tablespoons vegetable oil

1 teaspoon light soy sauce

1 tablespoon Chinese black vinegar

This recipe calls for fresh prawns but ready peeled frozen prawns can be used if need be. Just remember to defrost and pat dry if using frozen. The quantity of dried chilli sounds scary but they are not anywhere near as hot as fresh chillies. They impart a smokiness to the dish, but feel free to reduce the quantity if you wish.

—

Heat the vegetable oil in a wok over high heat. Swirl the wok around to coat in the oil. Add the dried chillies, spring onions, ginger and garlic and stir-fry for 20 seconds.

Add the prawns and stir-fry for 2–3 minutes until pink and almost cooked through.

Add the soy sauce and vinegar to the wok and stir-fry for a minute until the sauce thickly coats the prawns and they are cooked through.

Transfer to a serving platter and serve hot.

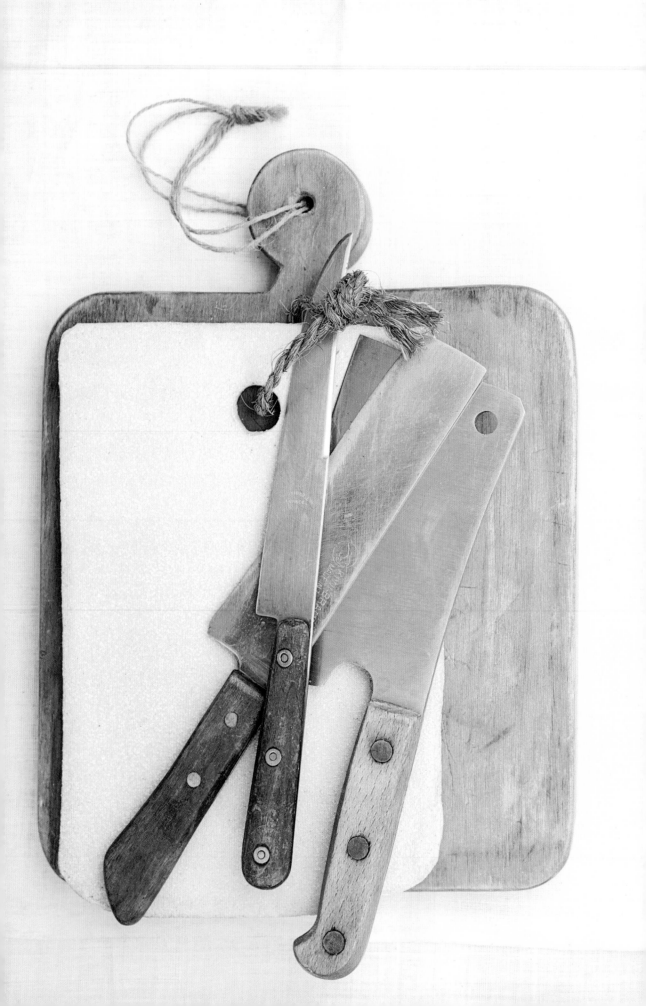

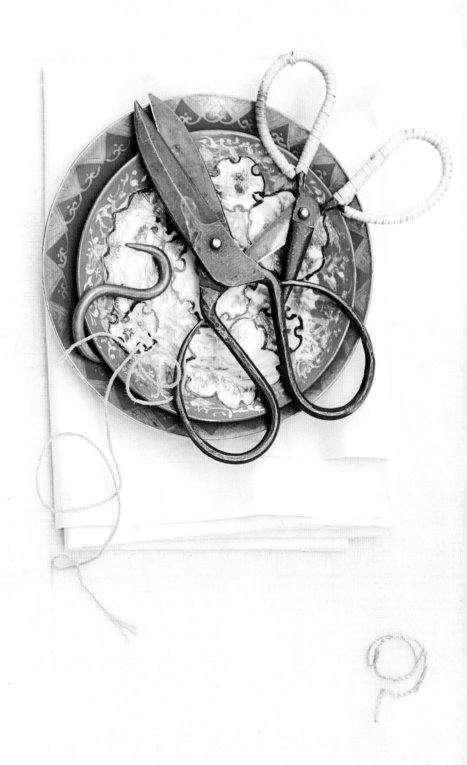

CHICKEN & DUCK

雞和鴨

SPICY CHICKEN SALAD

辣鷄沙律

SERVES: 4   *PREPARATION: 20 MINUTES*

FRESH

1 cooked rotisserie chicken, skin and meat shredded

1 red onion, finely sliced

1 Lebanese (short) cucumber, finely sliced

small bunch of coriander, leaves and stems roughly chopped

SPICES

1 teaspoon Szechuan peppercorns

1 teaspoon Chilli Salt (see page 212)

PANTRY

2 tablespoons light soy sauce

2 tablespoons sesame oil

While salads are not as common in Chinese cooking as in other Asian countries, they are just as tasty. Chilli does not dominate like it does in, say, Thai salads. Chinese salads are often more subtle in flavour, tempered with cooling cucumber, cabbage, tangy dressings and fresh herbs.

—

Put the Szechuan peppercorns in a small frying pan and cook over high heat until the peppercorns start to smoke. Tip into a bowl and leave to cool.

Grind the cool peppercorns in a spice mill to make a fine powder, then combine in a bowl with the Chilli Salt. Set aside.

Combine the cooked chicken, onion, cucumber and coriander in a large bowl.

Combine the soy sauce and sesame oil in a small bowl and pour over the salad.

Transfer to a large plate to serve. Serve the salt and pepper mix on the side to sprinkle over the salad.

LEMON CHICKEN

檸檬雞

SERVES: 4   *PREPARATION: 15 MINUTES*   *STANDING: 30 MINUTES*
COOKING: 10 MINUTES

FRESH

2 chicken breast fillets

120 ml freshly squeezed lemon juice

PANTRY

150 g self-raising flour

2 tablespoons caster sugar

1 teaspoon light soy sauce

75 g plain flour

vegetable oil, for frying

This dish pairs lightly battered fried chicken with a very tangy lemon-flavoured sauce. This savoury and sour combination is simply delicious and addictive.

—

Place the chicken between 2 layers of plastic wrap and pound it so it is an even 2 cm thickness all over. Refrigerate until needed.

Combine the self-raising flour and 180 ml cold water in a bowl. Stir to make a smooth batter, then set aside for 30 minutes.

Combine the lemon juice, sugar and soy sauce in a small saucepan. Cook over high heat until the mixture boils, stirring constantly. Boil for 1 minute until the sauce is thick and glossy. Remove from the heat.

Put the flour on a plate.

Half fill a wok with the vegetable oil and set over medium heat. The oil is ready when a cube of bread turns golden within 10–15 seconds.

Press the chicken breast into the flour so that it is coated all over. Dip the coated chicken in the batter, allowing any excess batter to drip off.

Carefully lower the chicken into the hot oil and cook for 4–5 minutes. Adjust the heat if the batter is browning too quickly. Turn the chicken over and cook for a further 4–5 minutes until the batter is golden and the chicken is cooked through.

Transfer the chicken to a plate lined with paper towel to absorb excess oil. Cut the chicken crossways into 1 cm slices and transfer to a serving plate. Quickly reheat the lemon sauce and pour over the chicken.

SIX WAYS WITH SESAME OIL
芝麻油的六種用法

❶ SESAME SOY NOODLES

Cook thin fresh egg noodles in boiling water for 2–3 minutes. Drain well. Add a generous splash of sesame oil and light soy sauce. Toss to combine, then transfer to a serving bowl. Sprinkle toasted sesame seeds over the noodles to serve.

❷ SESAME FRIED CHICKEN

Pour 240 ml sesame oil into a wok and heat over medium heat. Cut 2 skinless and boneless chicken breasts into large bite-sized pieces and toss in cornflour to coat all over. Fry the chicken for 4–5 minutes until golden. Scatter chopped coriander over the chicken and serve with Chilli Sauce (see page 210) on the side.

❸ TANGY SESAME SALAD

Whisk 2 tablespoons sesame oil, 1 tablespoon light soy sauce and 1 tablespoon Chinese black vinegar in a bowl. Pour the dressing over your favourite salad greens.

❹ SESAME, HONEY & MUSTARD DIPPING SAUCE

Stir 2 tablespoons sesame oil, 1 tablespoon honey, 1 tablespoon light soy sauce and 1 teaspoon hot mustard in a small bowl until well combined. Use as a dip for fried prawns and chicken.

❺ SESAME SOY CHICKEN WINGS

Preheat the oven to 180°C/Gas 4. Toss 12 chicken wings in a large bowl with 3 tablespoons sesame oil and 3 tablespoons soy sauce. Season. Tumble onto a baking tray lined with baking paper. Bake for about 40 minutes until golden and crisp. Serve with lemon wedges on the side.

❻ SESAME GRILLED ASPARAGUS

Snap off the woody asparagus ends from a bunch of asparagus and discard. Toss the asparagus spears in a bowl with 1 tablespoon sesame oil, 1 tablespoon light soy sauce and 1 tablespoon lemon juice. Tumble the asparagus onto a hot grill or into a hot wok and cook for 2 minutes on each side until golden. Sprinkle over toasted sesame seeds and serve hot.

THREE-CUP CHICKEN

三杯鷄

SERVES: 4   *PREPARATION: 10 MINUTES*   *COOKING: 15–20 MINUTES*

FRESH

6 chicken thigh fillets, each cut into
   three pieces

3 garlic cloves, unpeeled and smashed

3 cm piece fresh ginger, finely sliced

2 spring onions, finely sliced on
   the angle

PANTRY

2 tablespoons sesame oil

2 tablespoons Chinese rice wine

2 tablespoons light soy sauce

This recipe uses equal parts sesame oil, rice wine and soy sauce. The simplicity of this dish defies the flavour.

—

Combine the chicken, garlic, ginger and spring onions in a bowl and set aside.

Heat the sesame oil in a wok over high heat. Swirl around so the oil coats the wok.

Add the chicken mixture. Cook for 2 minutes, without stirring, so the chicken forms a golden crust.

Turn the chicken over and cook for a further 2 minutes, then stir-fry for a further minute, so all the ingredients are golden and the chicken is no longer pink.

Add the Chinese rice wine, soy sauce and 250 ml cold water. Stir to loosen any bits stuck to the bottom of the wok.

Bring to the boil, then reduce the heat so the sauce gently simmers. Cook for about 10–15 minutes until the mixture becomes dark and glossy and thickly coats the chicken. Transfer to a serving plate and serve hot with rice if liked.

HAINAN CHICKEN RICE

海南鷄飯

SERVES: 4   *PREPARATION: 10 MINUTES*   *COOKING: 1¼ HOURS*

FRESH

1 chicken, about 1.6 kg

5 cm piece fresh ginger,
    peeled and sliced

3 spring onions

1 quantity Ginger & Spring Onion
    Sauce (see page 210)

SPICES

2 tablespoons fine sea salt

PANTRY

300 g jasmine rice

This iconic dish is not only popular in China but also throughout South-east Asia. This is due to Chinese immigration and influence throughout the region. This is Chinese comfort food at its best.

—

Put the chicken in a large saucepan. Add enough cold water to cover, then add the sliced ginger, whole spring onions and salt.

Bring the water to the boil, then reduce the heat to a low simmer. Cook for 1 hour until the chicken is white and cooked through. Transfer the chicken to a chopping board and leave to rest while cooking the rice and the sauce.

Drain the cooking stock and reserve about 720 ml. The remaining stock may be kept warm and served with the chicken or saved and frozen for later use.

Wash the rice in a sieve under cold water until the water runs clear. Put the rice in a saucepan with the reserved stock and cook over high heat. When the stock is boiling rapidly, reduce the heat to low and cover the pan. Cook for 10 minutes. Remove from the heat and leave for 5 minutes until the rice is cooked. Leave covered to keep warm.

Chop the chicken Chinese-style (see pages 94–95) into 10–12 pieces. Serve the chicken with the rice and stock, if using, and the Ginger and Spring Onion Sauce on the side.

BANG BANG CHICKEN

棒棒雞

SERVES: 4   PREPARATION: 25 MINUTES   COOKING: 1¼ HOURS

FRESH

3 spring onions

2 skinless and boneless chicken
   breast fillets

2 cucumbers, finely sliced on the angle

small bunch coriander

PANTRY

70 g Chinese sesame paste (or
   smooth peanut butter)

1 tablespoon Chinese black vinegar

1 tablespoon honey

200 g bean thread vermicelli noodles

1 tablespoon toasted sesame seeds,
   to serve

**This is a popular and tasty street-food snack in the north of
China. Some say the name comes from the sound of chicken being
pounded to render the flesh easier to shred. It is the delicious
sauce with its combination of sesame paste, vinegar and honey
that distinguishes this recipe. Smooth peanut butter would make
a perfectly acceptable substitute for the sesame paste, but do
avoid using tahini.**

—

Cut the white parts from the spring onions and add to a saucepan
with 2 litres water. Finely slice the green parts of the spring onions
and set aside.

Bring the water to the boil. Add the chicken, cover the pan and
remove from the heat. Leave for 1 hour, then remove the chicken
from the pan.

When cool enough to handle, shred the chicken into thin, white
strands. Transfer to a large bowl and set aside.

Combine the sesame paste, vinegar and honey in a small bowl.
Add 60 ml boiling water and stir until smooth. Set aside.

Put the noodles in a heatproof bowl and cover with boiling water.
Leave for 10 minutes until soft. Rinse under cold water, then drain well.

Add the noodles to the chicken with the coriander, spring onions
and cucumbers. Toss the ingredients together until well combined.
Transfer to a serving plate, drizzle the sauce over and scatter with
sesame seeds.

TEA & SPICE SMOKED CHICKEN

茶香熏鶏

SERVES: 6–8   *PREPARATION: 10 MINUTES*   *RESTING: 1 HOUR*   *COOKING: 30 MINUTES*

FRESH

4 small skinless and boneless chicken breast fillets

Ginger & Spring Onion Sauce (see page 210), to serve

SPICES

1 quantity Five-spice (see page 213)

2 tablespoons coarse salt

PANTRY

50 g jasmine rice

20 g jasmine or green tea leaves

25 g light brown sugar

2 teaspoons light soy sauce

1 teaspoon sesame oil

This is a posh way to cook and present chicken. It does however create quite a bit of smoke in its preparation, so it is best done in a well-ventilated kitchen or outside on the barbecue.

—

Line the base of a wok with foil and line a bamboo steamer basket with baking paper.

Combine the Five-spice, rice, tea and sugar in a small bowl and scatter over the base of the wok.

Put the chicken in a bowl with the soy sauce and sesame oil and toss the chicken around. Sit the chicken in the bamboo steamer basket. Sit the steamer on a rack in the wok, so the steamer is not touching any part of the wok.

Put the wok over high heat. When the brown sugar mixture starts to smoke, cover the wok with a tight-fitting lid and smoke for 25 minutes, without removing the lid, until the chicken is golden. Turn off the heat and leave covered for 1 hour until the chicken is cooked through. Slice and serve with Ginger and Spring Onion Sauce on the side.

PEKING DUCK

北京鴨

SERVES: 8 AS A SHARED STARTER   *PREPARATION: 30 MINUTES*   *RESTING: 30 MINUTES*
COOKING: 1½ HOURS

FRESH

1 duck, about 2 kg, preferably with
neck intact

4 spring onions, white and green
parts separated

2 Lebanese (short) cucumbers, cut into
8 cm x 5 mm batons

1 quantity Peking Pancakes
(see page 216 or ready made)

SPICES

1 quantity Five-spice (see page 213)

PANTRY

2 tablespoons sesame oil

2 tablespoons dark soy sauce

3 tablespoons rice malt syrup

hoi sin sauce, to serve

This must be one of the most famous dishes to come out of China. Many recipes call for all sorts of tricky things to be done to the duck, but this one keeps it very simple. The breast meat is used for the pancakes; any remaining meat can be shredded and used in fried rice, salads, stir-fries and soups.

—

Preheat the oven to 220°C/Gas 7. Place a cooking rack over a baking dish and half fill the baking dish with water.

Tuck the neck and wing tips under the duck's body. Trim off and discard any excess fat around the cavity end of the duck. Insert the green parts of the spring onions and all the Five-spice into the cavity. Rub 1 tablespoon of the sesame oil over the skin of the duck.

Combine the remaining sesame oil, dark soy sauce and rice malt syrup in a small bowl and set aside.

Sit the duck on the rack and bake for 30 minutes. Reduce the oven temperature to 180°C/Gas 4. Brush the duck with some of the reserved sesame mixture and cook for a further 1 hour, brushing with the sesame mixture every 20 minutes until the skin is glossy and coffee coloured. Remove the duck and leave to rest for 30 minutes.

Cut off and discard the wing tips. Use a large cleaver or sharp knife to cut between the breasts and remove the breasts from the body of the duck. Reserve the remaining meat on the duck for later use. Slice the breast meat into thin strips and transfer to a serving platter.

Cut the white parts of the spring onions into 8 cm pieces. Arrange the spring onions, cucumbers, pancakes and hoi sin sauce on the serving platter with the duck to serve.

USE A CHINESE CLEAVER TO CHOP A WHOLE CHICKEN CHINESE-STYLE

如何使用中式厨刀以及如何用中式風格斬鷄

There are a few simple tricks to chop chicken Chinese-style. This technique is also a great way to cut up roast turkey.

Chinese cleaver

chopping board

Sit a cooked chicken, breast side up, on a clean chopping board.

1

Insert the cleaver or knife into the cavity of the chicken...

and firmly chop either side of the backbone.

Pull

out the backbone and discard.

2

Chop

between the two breasts to separate the bird into 2 halves.

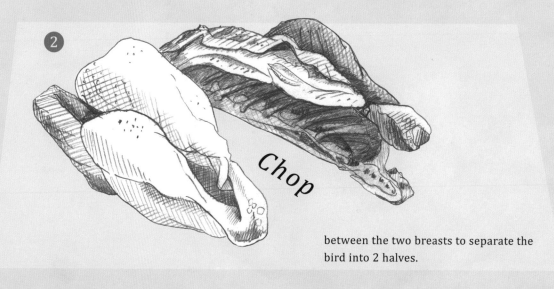

3

Cut off the wings, then cut off the wing tips.

Discard the wing tips.

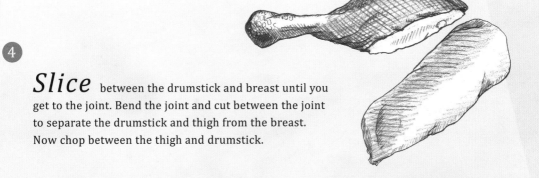

4

Slice between the drumstick and breast until you get to the joint. Bend the joint and cut between the joint to separate the drumstick and thigh from the breast. Now chop between the thigh and drumstick.

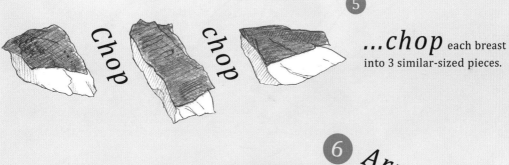

5

Chop *chop* *...chop* each breast into 3 similar-sized pieces.

6 *Arrange...*

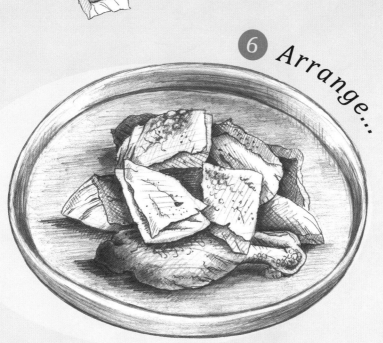

the bony cuts of the chopped chicken on a serving plate with the white breast meat on top.

RED-BRAISED CHICKEN

紅燒雞

SERVES: 4–6   *PREPARATION:* 10 MINUTES   *RESTING:* 1½ HOURS   *COOKING:* 1¾ HOURS

FRESH

10 cm piece fresh ginger, peeled and finely sliced

2 spring onions, roughly chopped

1 chicken, about 1.6 kg

Steamed Rice (see page 215), to serve

steamed green vegetables, to serve

SPICES

1 quantity Five-spice (see page 213)

PANTRY

3 tablespoons dark soy sauce

240 ml Chinese rice wine

50 g light brown sugar

This recipe uses the technique referred to as red braising. A large pot of water is seasoned with soy sauce, rice wine and sugar and made fragrant with the addition of five-spice. Chicken is gently poached in the aromatic mixture called a 'master stock', rendering the flesh tender and very tasty.

—

Combine the ginger, spring onions, Five-spice, dark soy sauce, rice wine and sugar in a large saucepan. Add 3 litres water and cook over high heat. Boil for 15 minutes for the flavours to develop.

Add the chicken, pushing it down so it is submerged in liquid. Cook for 15 minutes, then reduce the heat to low. Cover the pan and cook for 1 hour, until the chicken is cooked through. Remove from the heat and leave for an hour, covered.

Remove the chicken from the stock to a chopping board. Leave for 30 minutes to rest.

Strain the braising liquid and discard the spring onions and ginger. Pour 500 ml of the stock into a small saucepan and bring to the boil. Reduce the heat to a simmer and cook for 10–15 minutes until it has reduced by about half.

Cut the chicken into 10–12 pieces, Chinese-style (see pages 94–95) and transfer to a serving plate. Serve with the reduced braising liquid on the side and steamed rice and greens.

CRISPY CHICKEN WITH GINGER & SPRING ONION SAUCE

薑葱脆皮雞

SERVES: 4   PREPARATION: 15 MINUTES   RESTING: 1½ HOURS
CHILLING: 3-6 HOURS   COOKING: 1½ HOURS

FRESH

1 chicken, about 1.6 kg

Ginger & Spring Onion Sauce
    (see page 210), to serve

PANTRY

180 ml rice malt syrup

750 ml white vinegar

3 tablespoons light soy sauce

1 teaspoon sesame oil

To produce the distinctive crispy skin, the chicken is partially cooked in a vinegary sweet brine. It is then dried out in the fridge until the skin is taut and dry. The recipe calls for 3–6 hours drying time. For even crispier skin, the chicken could be left for 1–2 days in the fridge.

—

Combine 4 litres water with the rice malt syrup, vinegar and soy sauce in a large saucepan. Bring to the boil over high heat.

Add the chicken, making sure it is totally submerged. Cover and cook for 15 minutes. Remove from the heat and leave covered for 1 hour.

Transfer the chicken to a rack set over a large plate or tray. Refrigerate for 3–6 hours, so the skin dries out.

Preheat the oven to 180°C/Gas 4 and line a baking tray with baking paper.

Brush the sesame oil over the chicken. Sit the chicken on the tray and cook in the oven for 1¼ hours until the skin is crispy and golden. Transfer to a chopping board and leave to rest for 30 minutes.

Chop the chicken Chinese-style (see pages 94–95). Transfer all the chicken to a heatproof serving plate and serve with the Ginger and Spring Onion Sauce.

KUNG PAO CHICKEN

宮保雞丁

SERVES: 4   PREPARATION: 10 MINUTES   MARINATING: 15 MINUTES
COOKING: 10 MINUTES

FRESH

6 chicken thigh fillets, each cut into
   4 pieces

6 spring onions, cut into 5 cm lengths

3 cm piece fresh ginger, peeled and
   finely sliced

3 garlic cloves, smashed

SPICES

6 medium dried chillies

PANTRY

2 tablespoons oyster sauce

3 tablespoons vegetable oil

2 tablespoons Chinese black vinegar

50 g raw peanuts, lightly toasted,
roughly chopped

This may be one of the tastiest and most addictive Chinese dishes. It has a simple yet complex sauce of salty, sweet, sour and spicy flavours, with extra savoury and crunch factors provided by the addition of peanuts.

—

Combine the chicken and 1 tablespoon of the oyster sauce in a bowl. Set aside for 15 minutes.

Heat 2 tablespoons of the oil in a wok over high heat, swirling the wok around to coat in the oil. Add the chicken and cook for 2 minutes without stirring. Shake the wok to loosen any stuck-on bits and stir-fry for a further 2 minutes until the chicken is golden. Transfer the chicken to a bowl.

Heat the remaining oil in the wok over high heat. Add the spring onions, ginger, garlic and chillies and stir-fry for a minute until aromatic but not burning.

Return the chicken to the wok and stir-fry to combine. Add the remaining oyster sauce, vinegar and half the peanuts and stir-fry for 2–3 minutes until well combined. Transfer to a serving plate and scatter the remaining peanuts over the chicken.

SHANG TUNG CHICKEN

上湯滑鷄

SERVES: 4   *PREPARATION: 10 MINUTES*   *CHILLING: 3–6 HOURS*   *COOKING: 35 MINUTES*

FRESH

2 large chicken breasts, skin on

2 large red chillies, thinly sliced on
 the angle

small bunch coriander,
 roughly chopped

PANTRY

1 tablespoon sesame oil

3 tablespoons rice vinegar

2 tablespoons light soy sauce

2 teaspoons granulated sugar

This is a very simplified version of a delicious dish. The recipe calls for chicken breast with the skin on but you could use chicken thighs or the Maryland cut (drumstick and thigh). Remove the skin if you like, but it really does add so much more flavour.

—

Wash and pat dry the chicken, and put into a large bowl.

Combine the sesame oil, rice vinegar, soy sauce and sugar in a bowl, stirring so the sugar dissolves.

Pour 2 tablespoons of the mixture over the chicken and rub into the skin. Cover and refrigerate for 3–6 hours, turning the chicken every 30 minutes.

Put the remaining sesame oil mixture in a small saucepan and set aside. Preheat the oven to 220°C/Gas 7.

Sit the chicken, skin side up, on a baking tray lined with baking paper. Cook for 20 minutes, until the skin starts to turn golden.

Reduce the temperature to 160°C/Gas 3 and cook for a further 10 minutes until the chicken is golden and cooked through. Transfer the chicken to a chopping board and rest for 10 minutes. Chop the chicken crossways into 4 pieces and arrange on a serving platter.

Cook the sesame sauce mixture over medium heat until bubbling and pour over the chicken. Scatter the red chillies and coriander over the chicken to serve.

CLAY POT CHICKEN WITH CHINESE SAUSAGE & MUSHROOM

臘腸蘑菇石鍋雞

SERVES: 4   PREPARATION: 15 MINUTES   STANDING: 30 MINUTES
COOKING: 25 MINUTES

FRESH

3 skinless and boneless chicken thigh
    fillets, each cut into 4 pieces

2 spring onions, white and green parts
    finely sliced and separated

5 cm piece fresh ginger, peeled and
    finely sliced

PANTRY

1 tablespoon oyster sauce

6 medium dried shiitake mushrooms

300 g jasmine rice

2 Chinese sausages (*lap cheong*),
    finely sliced

**Clay pot cooking is convenient and produces very tasty results.
All the flavours are trapped inside the pot, ready to be released
when the lid is lifted at the dining table.**

—

Combine the chicken and oyster sauce in a bowl. Cover and set aside
for 30 minutes.

Meanwhile, put the mushrooms in a heatproof bowl. Pour over enough
boiling water to cover and leave for 30 minutes until the mushrooms
are soft. Drain and reserve 120 ml of the soaking liquid. Trim off the
stems and discard. Cut each cap into quarters and set aside.

Wash the rice in several changes of cold water until the water runs
clear. Drain well and put the rice in a 20 cm clay pot or saucepan. Add
600 ml cold water and place over high heat. When the water boils and
forms bubbling holes in the rice, reduce the heat to low and cover.
Cook for 10 minutes, until most of the water has evaporated.

Scatter the chicken and the marinade over the rice. Put the
mushrooms and sausage on top of the chicken, then scatter with the
spring onions and ginger. Cover and cook for 10 minutes until the
chicken is cooked through.

CHICKEN & ALMOND STIR-FRY

清炒杏仁鷄丁

SERVES: 4   PREPARATION: 10 MINUTES   MARINATING: 15 MINUTES
COOKING: 10 MINUTES

FRESH

2 skinless and boneless chicken breast fillets, cut into 2 cm pieces

2 spring onions, finely sliced

2 garlic cloves, finely chopped

5 cm piece fresh ginger, peeled and finely chopped

2 celery sticks, finely sliced, plus leaves roughly chopped

PANTRY

3 tablespoons oyster sauce

1 tablespoon vegetable oil

50 g toasted almonds

2 tablespoons Chinese rice wine

Celery gives an extra savoury note to any dish. Here, the celery remains crisp and crunchy. Combined with the almonds, this stir-fry provides lots of flavour and texture.

—

Combine the chicken in a bowl with 2 tablespoons of the oyster sauce. Toss the chicken around so it is coated in the sauce. Set aside for 15 minutes.

Heat the oil in a wok over high heat. Swirl the wok around so it is coated in the oil. Add the spring onions, garlic and ginger and stir-fry for just a few seconds.

Add the chicken and cook, without stirring, for 2 minutes. Stir-fry all the ingredients together for 2 minutes until well combined and the chicken is golden.

Add the celery and almonds and stir-fry for 2 minutes until well combined, but leaving the celery crisp.

Add the rice wine and the remaining oyster sauce to the wok. Stir-fry for a minute or two until well combined and the chicken is cooked through. Transfer to a serving plate and serve hot.

CHICKEN, CHILLI & BLACK BEAN STIR-FRY

豆豉香辣鷄塊

SERVES: 4   PREPARATION: 15 MINUTES   CHILLING: 3–6 HOURS   COOKING: 10 MINUTES

FRESH

6 skinless and boneless chicken thigh
  fillets, each cut into 4 pieces

1 red onion, sliced into thin wedges

1 large green capsicum (pepper),
  cut into thin strips

2 large red chillies, finely sliced on
  the angle

handful coriander leaves, to garnish

PANTRY

3 tablespoons Chinese rice wine

80 ml black bean sauce

1 tablespoon vegetable oil

Black beans are partially dried and fermented soy beans. They will keep for ages stored in an airtight bag or container. It is worth a trip to an Asian specialty food store to get a supply of these tasty treasures. If you have trouble finding them, look for a good quality, ready-made black bean sauce at the supermarket.

—

Put the chicken pieces in a bowl with 1 tablespoon of the rice wine and 2 tablespoons of the black bean sauce. Cover and refrigerate for 3–6 hours, for the flavours to develop. Drain the chicken pieces and discard the marinade.

Heat the oil in a wok over high heat, swirling the wok around to coat in the oil. Add the chicken pieces and cook for 2 minutes without stirring, so the chicken sizzles and turns golden.

Turn the chicken over and cook for another 2 minutes. Shake the wok to loosen any stuck-on bits of chicken and stir-fry for a minute. Use a slotted spoon or tongs to remove the chicken to a plate.

Allow the wok to reheat. Add the onion, capsicum and chilli and stir-fry for 2 minutes, so the vegetables are just tender. Return the chicken to the wok, then pour the remaining rice wine around the edge of the wok and stir to combine.

Stir in the remaining black bean sauce and 1 tablespoon water and cook for a minute or so until everything is well combined and hot. Transfer to a serving plate and scatter with the coriander.

MEAT
肉類

BARBECUE SPARE RIBS

BBQ排骨仔

SERVES: 4   PREPARATION: 15 MINUTES   CHILLING: 3-6 HOURS
COOKING: 1½ HOURS

FRESH

1 kg pork ribs

SPICES

1 teaspoon Five-spice (see page 213)

½ teaspoon ground black pepper

PANTRY

2 tablespoons char siu sauce (Chinese barbecue sauce)

1 tablespoon Chinese rice wine

2 tablespoons honey

2 teaspoons sesame oil

This simply delicious and easy recipe requires very little preparation. The ribs can be marinated for up to 2 days in advance. Although not traditionally Chinese, beef ribs could be used as an alternative.

—

Cut between the ribs to separate and put into a bowl.

Combine the Five-spice, black pepper, char siu sauce, rice wine, honey and sesame oil in a small bowl.

Pour over the ribs and toss the ribs around to coat all over in the sauce. Cover and refrigerate for 3–6 hours, turning every hour or so.

Preheat the oven to 180°C/Gas 4 and line a baking dish with baking paper.

Tumble the ribs and the marinade onto the tray and cook for about 45 minutes. Turn the ribs over and cook for a further 30 minutes. Increase the oven temperature to 220°C/Gas 7.

Turn ribs over again and cook for a further 15–20 minutes until the ribs are dark and glossy. Transfer to a serving plate and serve with steamed rice.

CHAR SIU

叉燒

SERVES: 6–8 TO SHARE   *PREPARATION:* 10 MINUTES   *MARINATING:* 6–8 HOURS
RESTING: 30 MINUTES   *COOKING:* 2¼ HOURS

FRESH

750 g pork neck, in one piece

SPICES

1 teaspoon Five-spice (see page 213)

PANTRY

50 g light brown sugar

3 tablespoons plum sauce

1 tablespoon dark soy sauce

2 tablespoons tomato sauce

1 tablespoon sesame oil

Char siu, or Chinese barbecued pork, is not actually cooked on the barbecue. Rather, the 'barbecue' refers to the flavour and texture of the cooked meat – very sweet, glossy and sticky! Any leftovers can be used in fried rice and noodle dishes.

—

Cut the pork in half lengthways. Put into a non-metallic bowl.

Combine the Five-spice, sugar, plum sauce, dark soy sauce, tomato sauce and sesame oil in a bowl. Pour over the pork, and use your hands to massage the sauce mixture into the meat. Cover and refrigerate for 6 hours, or overnight, turning the pork every 3 hours.

Preheat the oven to 220°C/Gas 7 and line a baking tray with baking paper.

Lay the pork on the tray and scrape out all the marinade over the pork. Cook in the oven for 20 minutes. Turn the meat over and cook for a further 20 minutes.

Reduce the oven temperature to 160°C/Gas 3 and cook for 1½ hours, turning every 20 minutes or so and basting with the pan juices, until the pork is dark and caramelised.

Transfer to a plate and cover with foil for 30 minutes before slicing.

CRISPY FIVE-SPICE PORK BELLY

香脆五香肚尖

SERVES: 4–6 TO SHARE   *PREPARATION: 20 MINUTES*   *CHILLING: 3–6 HOURS*
RESTING: 20–30 MINUTES   *COOKING: 1½ HOURS*

FRESH

1 kg pork belly, skin on and boneless

SPICES

1 tablespoon Five-spice Salt
  (see page 213)

½ teaspoon ground white pepper

1 teaspoon fine sea salt

PANTRY

1 teaspoon caster sugar

1 teaspoon rice vinegar

You can find pork belly with skin on at some supermarkets, or alternatively at a Chinese butcher. This is a simple recipe producing pork that is both addictively crispy and unctuous. Cold leftovers are delicious thinly sliced and added to fried rice.

—

Combine the Five-spice Salt, sugar and white pepper in a small bowl and set aside.

Wash the pork and pat dry. Put the pork on a chopping board with the skin side down. Cut deep slices into the flesh of the pork, 1.5 cm apart and 1 cm deep, but not cutting through to the skin. Rub the spice mixture all over the meat and into the cuts, but not on the skin.

Combine the salt and vinegar in a small bowl. Brush a little over the skin of the pork. Reserve the rest to use later. Refrigerate for 3–6 hours.

Preheat the oven to 220°C/Gas 7 and line a baking tray with foil.

Sit the pork, skin side up, on the tray and pat the skin dry with paper towel. Brush with some more of the salt and vinegar mix. Cook for 30 minutes. Reduce the heat to 180°C/Gas 4 and cook for 1 hour until golden and crispy. Rest for 20–30 minutes.

To cut the pork, place skin side down on a chopping board. Use a cleaver or large knife to cut where the initial cuts were made, chopping through the crispy skin. Now cut each slice into large bite-sized pieces. Serve warm with steamed rice and Chinese greens.

MU SHU PORK

木須肉

SERVES: 4   PREPARATION: 20 MINUTES   MARINATING: 15 MINUTES
COOKING: 10 MINUTES

FRESH

400 g pork scotch fillet, finely sliced

2 eggs, beaten

3 spring onions, cut into 5 cm lengths

2 large red chillies, finely sliced

1 quantity Peking Pancakes
  (see page 216)

PANTRY

2 tablespoons hoi sin sauce

20 g dried black fungus

2 tablespoons vegetable oil

This recipe is typical of Northern-style Chinese dishes, which incorporate slivers of sweetly flavoured stir-fried meat wrapped in a warm, soft pancake. Wheat-based breads, buns, pancakes and noodles are more common in the north of China.

—

Combine the pork and 1 tablespoon of the hoi sin sauce in a bowl. Set aside for 15 minutes.

Meanwhile, put the dried fungus in a small heatproof bowl and add 250 ml boiling water. Soak for 15 minutes. Drain the fungus and reserve 2 tablespoons of the soaking liquid.

Heat 1 tablespoon of the oil in a wok over high heat. Swirl the wok around to coat in the oil. Add the eggs and leave them to cook for about 1 minute until they start to puff up and set firm around the edges. Stir the eggs from the outside in and cook until just set. Transfer the cooked eggs to a plate and wipe the wok clean.

Heat the remaining oil in the wok over high heat. Swirl the oil around to coat the wok.

Add the spring onions and chillies. Stir-fry for 1–2 minutes until softened. Add the pork and stir-fry for 2–3 minutes until the pork is golden brown. Stir in the soaked fungus, soaking liquid and the remaining hoi sin sauce. Stir-fry for 1 minute until well combined. Add the scrambled eggs and stir through.

Transfer to a serving plate. Serve with pancakes on the side.

MA PO TOFU

麻婆豆腐

SERVES: 4   *PREPARATION: 10 MINUTES*   *COOKING: 15 MINUTES*

FRESH

1 tablespoon finely grated fresh ginger

2 garlic cloves, finely chopped

1 spring onion, white and green parts finely sliced and separated

300 g minced pork

300 g soft tofu, well drained and cut into small cubes

SPICES

ground Szechuan peppercorns, to serve

PANTRY

1 tablespoon vegetable oil

2 tablespoons Chinese chilli bean sauce

360 ml chicken stock

This is a signature dish from the Szechuan province of China. A ubiquitous ingredient in the cooking from this area is *tobian jian* – chilli bean sauce – and it is finished off with a sprinkling of mouth-numbing ground Szechuan peppercorns.

—

Heat the oil in a wok over high heat. Swirl the wok around to coat in the oil. Add the ginger, garlic and the white parts of the spring onion and stir-fry for 20 seconds.

Add the pork and stir-fry for 4–5 minutes until well browned. Stir in the chilli bean sauce and then the stock. Add the tofu.

Reduce the heat to medium and simmer for about 10 minutes until the liquid has almost evaporated. Transfer to a large bowl and scatter with the green parts of the spring onion and ground Szechuan peppercorns to serve.

CHAIRMAN MAO'S PORK

毛氏紅燒肉

SERVES: 6 TO SHARE   *PREPARATION: 20 MINUTES*   *COOKING: ABOUT 2 HOURS*

FRESH

1 kg pork belly, skin on and boneless,
in one piece

5 cm piece fresh ginger, peeled and
finely sliced

2 spring onions, white and green parts
finely sliced and separated

SPICES

1 quantity Five-spice (see page 213)

PANTRY

2 tablespoons vegetable oil

2 tablespoons white sugar

3 tablespoons Chinese rice wine

3 tablespoons dark soy sauce

2 tablespoons light soy sauce

This dish comes from Mao's home province of Hunan. It is said to have been Mao's favourite meal and subsequently named after him. This recipe also incorporates 'red braising' even though it is not red. It is said that red brings luck, good fortune and joy.

—

Bring a large saucepan of water to the boil. Add the pork, cover and cook for 5 minutes. This helps to remove the impurities in the meat.

Drain, discard the water and transfer the pork to a chopping board. When cool enough to handle chop crossways into 3 cm strips, then cut into 3 cm wide pieces. Set aside.

Combine the vegetable oil and sugar in a wok. Cook over high heat until the mixture sizzles. Reduce the heat to medium and cook for 2–3 minutes until the mixture turns toffee coloured.

Carefully add the rice wine to the wok. It will splutter as it hits the hot sugar mixture. Stir to combine then add 1 litre water, both soy sauces, the ginger, the white parts of the spring onions, the Five-spice and the pork. Bring to the boil, then reduce the heat to a low simmer. Cover and cook for 1½ hours until the pork is very tender.

Use a slotted spoon or tongs to remove the pork to a serving plate. Increase the heat to high and cook the sauce for 10 minutes until thickened and syrupy. Pour about 250 ml of the sauce over the pork and scatter with some of the finely sliced spring onion greens.

STIR-FRIED BEEF & BROCCOLI WITH OYSTER SAUCE

耗油西蘭花炒牛肉

SERVES: 4   PREPARATION: 10 MINUTES   MARINATING: 30 MINUTES   COOKING: 10 MINUTES

FRESH

600 g fillet steak, thinly sliced across the grain

200 g broccoli, cut into small florets

2 garlic cloves, chopped

5 cm piece fresh ginger, peeled and grated

PANTRY

3 teaspoons light soy sauce

2 tablespoons vegetable oil

3 tablespoons oyster sauce

This dish typifies what many people associate with Chinese cookery – fresh ingredients, simply prepared and cooked quickly. More specifically, this type of stir-fry defines the cooking from South-east China and Hong Kong.

—

Combine the meat in a bowl with 2 teaspoons of the soy sauce. Cover and set aside for 30 minutes.

Put the broccoli in a heatproof bowl. Pour over enough boiling water to cover. Leave for 2 minutes until the broccoli is tender and bright green. Rinse under cold water and drain well. Set aside.

Heat a wok or large frying pan over high heat. Add the oil and swirl around to coat the wok or pan in the oil.

Add the beef and spread the meat out in a single layer. Cook for 3 minutes, without stirring. Now stir-fry the meat for 1 minute until it is brown. Add the garlic and ginger and stir-fry for 1 minute.

Add the broccoli, remaining soy sauce and the oyster sauce and stir to combine. Serve hot with rice.

SIX WAYS WITH HOI SIN SAUCE

海鮮醬的六種用法

❶ HOI SIN ROASTED CHICKEN

Preheat the oven to 180°C/Gas 4. Rub 3 tablespoons hoi sin sauce all over the skin of a whole roasting chicken. Sit on a baking rack set over a baking dish. Bake for 1¼ hours until the juices run clear when the chicken is pierced. Leave to cool, then chop the chicken, Chinese-style (see pages 94–95).

❷ HOI SIN PORK SKEWERS

Chop pork fillet into bite-sized cubes and thread onto bamboo skewers that have been soaked in cold water for 30 minutes. Brush the pork with enough hoi sin sauce to coat. Cook under a hot grill until golden and the pork is cooked through.

❸ HOI SIN CHICKEN WINGS

Preheat the oven to 180°C/Gas 4. Toss chicken wings in a bowl with enough hoi sin sauce so they are coated all over. Bake for 40 minutes until golden and cooked through.

❹ HOI SIN DIPPING SAUCE

Place 3 tablespoons hoi sin sauce, 1 tablespoon peanut butter and 1 teaspoon dark soy sauce in a bowl. Mix until smooth and well combined. Use as a dip for fried spring rolls, prawns or chicken.

❺ HOI SIN DRESSING

Whisk 3 tablespoons hoi sin sauce with a splash of orange juice and a drizzle of sesame oil in a small bowl until well combined. Use as a dressing for your favourite greens, chicken or seafood salad.

❻ HOI SIN BAKED PRAWNS

Preheat the oven to 180°C/Gas 4. Toss 24 frozen ready peeled large prawns with 3 tablespoons hoi sin sauce so the prawns are coated all over in the sauce. Sprinkle with chilli flakes and ground black pepper. Bake until the prawns are pink and curled up. Serve hot.

STIR-FRIED BEEF & CAPSICUM WITH BLACK BEAN SAUCE

耗油西蘭花炒牛肉

SERVES: 4   *PREPARATION: 10 MINUTES*   *MARINATING: 30 MINUTES*
COOKING: ABOUT 10 MINUTES

FRESH

500 g fillet or rump steak, finely sliced
  across the grain

2 garlic cloves, finely chopped

1 large green capsicum (pepper)

2 spring onions, cut into 3–4 cm lengths

PANTRY

3 tablespoons Chinese rice wine

2 tablespoons vegetable oil

2 tablespoons Chinese black beans,
  mashed with a fork

The savoury or umami flavour of black beans makes anything they are cooked with taste even better. But it's not just meats that go with black beans. Slivers of black bean can be scattered on fresh seafood before being steamed.

—

Put the beef and garlic in a bowl. Add 1 tablespoon of the rice wine. Use your hands or kitchen tongs to toss the ingredients around in the bowl. Cover and set aside for 30 minutes.

To prepare the capsicum, stand it upright and cut each of the four sides off. Scrape off the white membrane and any seeds and discard. Roughly chop the capsicum into triangle shapes. Put into a bowl with the spring onions and set aside.

Heat the oil in a wok over high heat. Swirl the wok around so it is coated in the oil. When the oil is very hot, add the capsicum and spring onions. Stir-fry for 1–2 minutes until the capsicum just starts to blister and is glossy. Use a slotted spoon to remove to a bowl.

Allow the oil in the wok to reheat. Add all the beef mixture to the wok. Leave for 2 minutes, without stirring, so the beef forms a dark golden crust. Stir-fry for another minute until the beef is no longer pink.

Add the black beans to the wok with the capsicum and spring onions. Stir-fry to combine with the beef.

Add the remaining rice wine and stir-fry so it sizzles and evaporates. Stir in the black bean sauce and cook for just a minute, so it is heated through. Transfer to a serving plate and serve hot with rice.

FRAGRANT BEEF HOT POT

麻辣牛肉香鍋

SERVES: 4   *PREPARATION: 15 MINUTES*   *COOKING: ABOUT 1¾ HOURS*

FRESH

500 g chuck steak, cut into 3 cm pieces

1 onion, thinly sliced

2 garlic cloves, chopped

5 cm piece fresh ginger, peeled and
finely sliced into rounds

SPICES

1 quantity Five-spice (see page 213)

sea salt and ground white pepper

PANTRY

1 tablespoon vegetable oil

8 medium dried shiitake mushrooms

2 teaspoons dark soy sauce

**A Chinese clay pot is an inexpensive investment to have in
your kitchen. However, a casserole or any other heavy-based
ovenproof dish will do. Cooking in a clay pot will create
anticipation as the lid is lifted at the table, releasing all the
wonderful flavours hidden within.**

—

Heat the oil in a frying pan over high heat. Add the beef, onion, garlic
and ginger and stir-fry for 4–5 minutes until the beef is brown and
the onion has softened a little.

Transfer the mixture to a heatproof clay pot. Add 750 ml water,
Five-spice, mushrooms and soy sauce.

Season with sea salt and ground white pepper. Bring to the boil, then
cover and cook over low heat for 1½ hours until the meat is very
tender. Serve with steamed rice or noodles.

STIR-FRIED LAMB WITH LEEKS, CUMIN & BLACK VINEGAR

孜然羊肉

SERVES: 4   PREPARATION: 15 MINUTES   MARINATING: 30 MINUTES
COOKING: 10 MINUTES

FRESH

500 g lamb fillet, cut into 3 cm pieces

2 leeks

2 tablespoons Chilli Sauce
  (see page 210)

SPICES

2 teaspoons ground cumin

PANTRY

3 tablespoons Chinese black vinegar

2 tablespoons vegetable oil

Lamb is a common ingredient in North-western Chinese cooking. It is used in stir-fries, soups, dumplings and pies. This simple but very tasty stir-fry exemplifies the cooking of this region. It may seem odd but cumin is a spice that is used in Chinese cooking and it pairs very well with lamb.

—

Combine the lamb in a bowl with 1 tablespoon of the black vinegar and the cumin. Cover and set aside for 30 minutes.

Cut off the green tops and root end from the leeks and discard. Cut the white part in half lengthways and wash if need be to remove any dirt. Cut into thick slices and set aside.

Heat 1 tablespoon of the oil in a wok over high heat. Swirl the wok around to coat in the oil. Add the leeks and stir-fry for 2 minutes until silky and tender. Remove to a bowl.

Add the remaining oil to the wok. When smoking hot, use a slotted spoon to transfer the lamb to the wok, reserving the marinade. Cook for 2 minutes without stirring. Shake the wok and stir-fry for another minute until the lamb is brown all over.

Return the leeks to the wok. Add the Chilli Sauce, the remaining vinegar and the reserved marinade and stir-fry for 2 minutes. Serve hot with rice or noodles.

NORTHERN-STYLE ROASTED LAMB PANCAKES

北方羊肉煎餅

SERVES: 4   *PREPARATION: 15 MINUTES*   *RESTING: 30 MINUTES*   *COOKING: 1¾ HOURS*

FRESH

1 kg boneless lamb shoulder

2 Lebanese (short) cucumbers, shredded

3 spring onions, cut into thin matchsticks

1 quantity Peking Pancakes (see page 216)

PANTRY

2 teaspoons sesame oil

3 tablespoons hoi sin sauce

10 g dried black fungus

80 g vermicelli noodles

Lamb is commonly used in the north of China in stir-fries and dumplings and often spiked with cumin, a spice we don't typically associate with Chinese food. Here, the lamb is slow cooked, rendering it fork tender so it can be shredded and wrapped in warm pancakes.

—

Preheat the oven to 180°C/Gas 4.

Combine 1 teaspoon of the sesame oil and 1 tablespoon of the hoi sin sauce in a small bowl. Rub all over the lamb.

Transfer the lamb to a snug fitting baking tray and pour 125 ml water into the tray. Cook for 1½ hours until the meat is dark golden. Remove to a plate and cover with foil for 30 minutes. Finely slice the lamb and transfer to a serving plate.

Put the fungus in a heatproof bowl. Add boiling water to cover and leave for 15 minutes. Drain well and roughly chop.

Put the noodles in a heatproof bowl. Add boiling water to cover and leaves for 10 minutes until the noodles are soft. Rinse under cold water and drain well.

Combine the fungus and noodles in a bowl. Add the remaining sesame oil, cucumbers and spring onions and toss to combine. Transfer to a serving bowl or plate.

To serve, spread a small amount of the remaining hoi sin sauce on a pancake. Top with some lamb and the noodle salad and fold.

VEGETABLES & TOFU

蔬菜和豆腐

CANTONESE PICKLED VEGETABLES

廣東泡菜

SERVES: 8 TO SHARE   *PREPARATION: 15 MINUTES*   *RESTING: 2 HOURS*   *CHILLING: 1 DAY*
COOKING: 15 MINUTES

FRESH

2 carrots, roughly chopped

100 g daikon radish, roughly chopped

2 Lebanese (short) cucumbers,
  halved or quartered lengthways and
  roughly chopped

8 red radishes, quartered

SPICES

2 tablespoons salt

PANTRY

750 ml rice wine vinegar

220 g white sugar

Chinese pickles are generally light, fresh and fast. The vegetables used here are a good starting point but as you become more familiar with the recipe, feel free to add whatever vegetables you like. Large seeded chillies, red onion and cabbage would work well using this pickling technique.

—

Put the carrot, daikon and cucumber in a bowl. Sprinkle the salt over the vegetables, toss to combine and set aside for 2 hours.

Transfer the salted vegetables to a colander and rinse under cold water. Shake to remove as much water as possible. Transfer to a bowl.

Combine the vinegar and sugar in a saucepan and bring to the boil. Reduce the heat and simmer for 10–15 minutes until syrupy. Leave to cool, then pour over the vegetables.

Add the red radishes and refrigerate for 1 day before eating.

How to:
BLANCH GREENS
如何漂洗蔬菜

One of the best ways to prepare Chinese greens is to quickly cook them
in boiling water (blanching). This method keeps the greens crisp and fresh.
Transfer the blanched greens to a serving plate and simply finish
off with your favourite sauce.

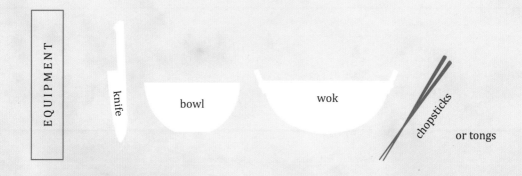

EQUIPMENT

knife   bowl   wok   chopsticks   or tongs

1

Snap off the woody ends from the stems
of the greens and discard.

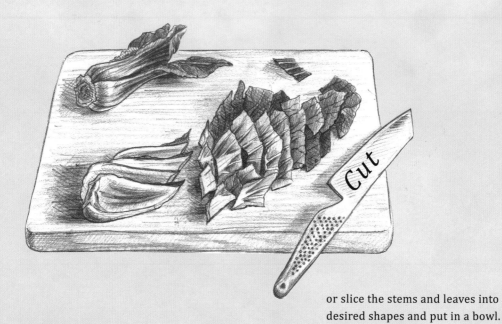

Cut

or slice the stems and leaves into
desired shapes and put in a bowl.

② *Half fill*

a wok with water and
bring to the boil.

③ *Tip*

the bowl of greens into the boiling water and use
large chopsticks or kitchen tongs to move the
greens around in the water.

Cook for 2–3 minutes, until the greens
are tender yet still vibrant in colour and crisp.

④ *Use tongs* or a wok spider to
remove the greens to a serving plate or platter.

Drizzle

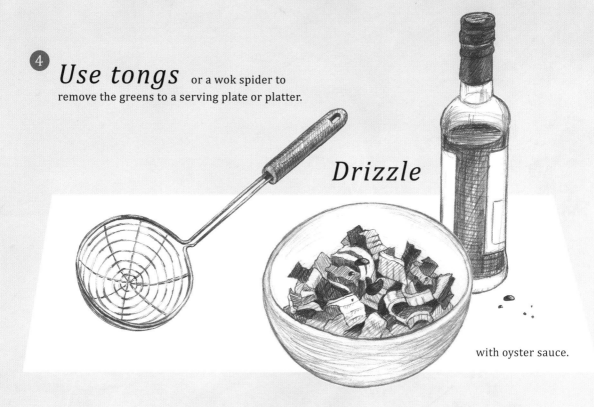

with oyster sauce.

FRIED TOFU WITH SPICED SALT

椒鹽豆腐

SERVES: 4   PREPARATION: 10 MINUTES   COOKING: 10 MINUTES

FRESH

600 g silken (soft) tofu, cut into
  2.5 cm cubes

1 large red chilli, finely chopped

1 spring onion, finely chopped

lemon wedges, to serve

SPICES

Chilli Salt (see page 212), to sprinkle

PANTRY

150 g plain flour

750 ml vegetable oil, for frying

This tofu recipe may well convert anyone to this pressed bean-curd product. It comes in several varieties, mostly based on texture, but can also come marinated or mildly spiced. Soft tofu needs to be used for this recipe. The outside forms a soft, golden crust enclosing a custard-like texture. It is all finished off with a dusting of chilli salt.

—

Put the tofu on a plate lined with several layers of paper towel for 10 minutes to absorb excess water.

Put the flour in a bowl.

Add the oil to a wok and heat over high heat. The oil is ready when a cube of bread turns golden in 10–15 seconds.

Working in batches, put a handful of tofu cubes in the flour and gently toss to coat. Shake off excess flour and fry for 2–3 minutes until golden. Transfer to a plate lined with paper towel. Repeat to cook all the tofu.

Serve on a plate, sprinkled with Chilli Salt to taste, and with the chopped chilli, spring onion and lemon wedges on the side.

TOMATO & BLACK FUNGUS WITH TANGY GLASS NOODLES

濃香三色沙律

SERVES: 4   *PREPARATION: 15 MINUTES*   *COOKING: 15 MINUTES*

FRESH

3 ripe tomatoes, cut into thin wedges

2 spring onions, finely sliced on
   the angle

small bunch coriander, leaves and
   stems roughly chopped

PANTRY

200 g vermicelli noodles

50 g dried black fungus

2 tablespoons Chinese black vinegar

2 tablespoons light soy sauce

1 tablespoon sesame oil

**These versatile glass noodles won't absorb too much liquid
so they are perfect to use in a salad with fresh vegetables
and a tangy dressing.**

—

Put the noodles in a heatproof bowl. Add enough boiling water to
cover. Leave for 10 minutes until softened. Rinse under cold water.
Drain well and set aside.

Put the fungus in a heatproof bowl. Add enough boiling water to
cover. Leave for 5 minutes until the mushrooms have expanded and
are soft. Drain well and finely slice. Combine in a bowl with the
tomatoes, spring onions and coriander.

Combine the vinegar, soy sauce and sesame oil in a small bowl and
pour over the salad. Toss to combine and transfer to a plate to serve.

SPICY GREEN BEAN STIR-FRY
乾煸四季豆

SERVES: 4   *PREPARATION: 15 MINUTES*   *COOKING: 15 MINUTES*

FRESH

300 g green beans, trimmed

5 cm piece fresh ginger, finely grated

2 garlic cloves, finely chopped

SPICES

1 teaspoon dried chilli flakes

PANTRY

vegetable oil, for frying

2 tablespoons Chinese rice wine

1 tablespoon light soy sauce

This is a great way to cook green beans. Simple flash frying keeps them crisp and locks in all the flavour.

—

Add enough oil to come one-third of the way up the side of a wok and set over high heat. When the surface of the oil is very hot and shimmering, carefully add a handful of beans and fry for 2–3 minutes until tender. Use a slotted spoon to remove the beans to a plate. Allow the oil to reheat and repeat the process until all the beans have been cooked.

Pour off all but 1 tablespoon of oil from the wok. Heat over high heat, swirling the wok around to coat in the oil. Add the ginger, garlic and chilli flakes and stir-fry for 20 seconds to flavour the oil but not allowing them to burn.

Add all the beans to the wok and stir-fry for 1 minute. Add the rice wine and soy sauce to the wok, pouring them in around the hot edges. Stir-fry for 1 minute until well combined, then transfer to a serving plate. Serve hot.

1 *choy sum*

4 *water spinach*

2 *baby bok choy*

CHINESE GREENS
中式蔬菜

3 *Chinese broccoli*

STIR-FRIED WATER SPINACH WITH FERMENTED BEAN CURD

腐乳空心菜

SERVES: 4   PREPARATION: 10 MINUTES   COOKING: 5 MINUTES

FRESH

large bunch water spinach
   (about 250 g)

1 garlic clove, finely chopped

5 cm piece fresh ginger, peeled and
   finely grated

PANTRY

1 tablespoon vegetable oil

2 tablespoons fermented bean curd

2 teaspoons light soy sauce

Water spinach is also known as morning glory or ong choy. It has tender leaves and stems that are delicious when briefly stir-fried. Here, it is flavoured with fermented bean curd which is the closest thing Chinese cuisine has to cheese. It has a tangy, umami taste.

—

Wash the water spinach and shake off any excess water. Cut into 10 cm lengths.

Heat the vegetable oil in a wok over high heat. Swirl the wok around to coat in the oil. Add the garlic and ginger and stir-fry for a few seconds to flavour the oil.

Add the bean curd and stir-fry for 1 minute, breaking up the bean curd with the back of a fork or spatula.

Add the water spinach and stir-fry for 2 minutes until wilted. Stir in the soy sauce and transfer to a serving plate. Serve hot as a side dish.

SIX WAYS WITH CHINESE BROCCOLI

芥蘭的六種做法

1 STIR-FRIED CHINESE BROCCOLI

Heat a splash of vegetable oil in a wok over high heat. Add 3 finely sliced garlic cloves and cook until golden and aromatic. Add a bunch of trimmed Chinese broccoli. Stir-fry for a couple of minutes until tender. Transfer to a serving plate and drizzle with light soy sauce.

2 STEAMED CHINESE BROCCOLI

Chop the woody ends off a bunch of Chinese broccoli and discard. Chop the bunch into thirds. Layer the broccoli on a heatproof plate with the stems on the bottom and leafy ends on top. Transfer to a bamboo steamer, cover and steam for 8–10 minutes until wilted. Drizzle with oyster sauce to serve.

3 NOODLES WITH SHREDDED CHINESE BROCCOLI

Shred the leaves and the fine stems of a bunch of Chinese broccoli. Cook with egg noodles until tender. Drain well and season with light soy sauce to taste.

4 STIR-FRIED BROCCOLI STEMS

Chop the thick, crunchy stems of Chinese broccoli and stir-fry with sesame oil and oyster sauce.

5 BLANCHED CHINESE BROCCOLI WITH FLOWERS

Blanch the leaves and stems of a bunch of Chinese broccoli with the flowers intact and drizzle with oyster sauce.

6 STEAMED FISH WRAPPED IN CHINESE BROCCOLI LEAVES

Steam fish or chicken fillets in a bamboo basket lined with whole Chinese broccoli leaves and serve with fresh Chilli Sauce (see page 210).

BUDDHA'S DELIGHT

羅漢齋

SERVES: 4   *PREPARATION:* 10 MINUTES   *COOKING:* 8–10 MINUTES

FRESH

bunch garlic chives, cut into
  2 cm lengths

400–500 g fresh shiitake mushrooms,
  torn in half

400 g tin baby corn, drained

200 g tin sliced bamboo
  shoots, drained

250 g bean sprouts, trimmed

375 g tofu puffs or firm tofu, cut into
  3 cm pieces

PANTRY

1 tablespoon vegetable oil

2 tablespoons oyster sauce

This is a very popular dish for Chinese Buddhists. Vegetarian oyster sauce is readily available in popular brands and could be used instead of normal oyster sauce to keep this strictly vegan. The tofu puffs are ready-fried tofu and can be bought from Asian food stores.

—

Heat the oil in a wok over high heat. Swirl the wok around to coat in the oil. Add the garlic chives and mushrooms and stir-fry for 2–3 minutes until the mushrooms are just tender.

Add the baby corn, bamboo shoots and bean sprouts and stir-fry until well combined.

Add the tofu puffs and pour in the oyster sauce and 2 tablespoons cold water around the edge of the wok. Stir-fry for 1 minute until all the ingredients are well combined and hot. Transfer to a serving plate and serve with rice or egg noodles.

STEAMED EGGPLANT WITH GINGER & CORIANDER

薑葱蒸茄子

SERVES: 4   PREPARATION: 10 MINUTES   COOKING: 20 MINUTES

FRESH

3 garlic cloves, crushed

1 large eggplant (aubergine)

handful chopped coriander

PANTRY

1 tablespoon light soy sauce

1 tablespoon Chinese black vinegar

½ teaspoon white sugar

1 teaspoon sesame oil

Most people might think that eggplant can only be fried or roasted. Here it is steamed, which is a very Chinese technique, rendering the flesh of the eggplant silky soft.

—

Half fill a wok with water and bring to the boil. Set a cooking rack inside the wok, ensuring it is above the water level.

Combine the garlic, soy sauce, black vinegar, sugar and sesame oil in a bowl. Set aside.

Peel the eggplant and cut into 5 x 1 cm strips. Arrange the eggplant on a heatproof plate that will fit inside a bamboo steamer basket.

Set the bamboo steamer on the cooking rack. Cover the wok and steam for 20 minutes until the eggplant is silky tender. Scatter with the coriander to serve.

STIR-FRIED POTATO WITH SOY, CHILLI & VINEGAR

醋溜土豆絲

SERVES: 4 *PREPARATION: 15 MINUTES* *DRYING: 2–3 HOURS* *COOKING: 15 MINUTES*

FRESH

4 medium waxy potatoes, peeled, washed and julienned

1 spring onion, white and green parts finely sliced and separated

SPICES

1 teaspoon dried chilli flakes

PANTRY

2 tablespoons vegetable oil

2 tablespoons Chinese black vinegar

1 tablespoon light soy sauce

This unusual recipe is delicious but relies on using a firm, waxy variety of potato. Floury potatoes will fall apart when stir-fried. The flavour is similar to salty chips with vinegar.

—

Bring a saucepan of water to the boil. Add the potatoes and cook for 5 minutes until tender and to remove excess starch. Rinse under cold water and drain well. Tumble the potatoes onto a baking tray. Set aside for 2–3 hours to completely dry out.

Heat the oil in a wok over high heat. Swirl the wok around to coat in the oil. Add the potatoes and the white parts of the spring onion and cook for 3–4 minutes without stirring. Shake the wok to loosen any stuck-on bits and stir-fry for 2 minutes, until the potatoes are golden and glossy.

Add the vinegar and soy sauce to the wok by pouring around the hot edges. Sprinkle the chilli flakes over the potatoes and stir-fry for 1 minute until well combined. Transfer to a serving plate and scatter with the green parts of the spring onion to serve.

STIR-FRIED ASPARAGUS, BABY CORN & SNOW PEAS

蘆筍玉米炒豌豆

SERVES: 4   *PREPARATION: 15 MINUTES*   *COOKING: 10 MINUTES*

FRESH

2 bunches asparagus, ends trimmed
and sliced on the angle

400 g baby corn, halved on the angle

200 g snow peas (mangetout), trimmed
and cut into thin strips

3 garlic cloves, smashed

3 cm piece fresh ginger, peeled and
finely sliced

PANTRY

2 tablespoons vegetable oil

2 tablespoons light soy sauce

A wok can struggle to stay hot when there are too many ingredients. A simple tip is to blanch the vegetables prior to cooking. This will make the stir-frying easy and quick.

—

Bring a large saucepan of water to the boil. Add the asparagus, corn and snow peas. Turn off the heat and leave for 2 minutes until the vegetables are just tender. Rinse under cold water and drain well. Set aside.

Heat the oil in a wok over high heat, swirling the wok around to coat in the oil. Add the garlic and ginger and stir-fry for just 20 seconds to flavour the oil but not allow the mixture to burn.

Add all the vegetables and stir-fry for 3–4 minutes.

Add the soy sauce to the wok by pouring in around the hot edges. Stir-fry for 1 minute and transfer to a serving plate.

STIR-FRIED CHINESE CABBAGE, MUSHROOMS & BEAN SPROUTS

白菜小菇炒豆芽

SERVES: 4   *PREPARATION: 15 MINUTES*   *COOKING: 10 MINUTES*

FRESH

5 cm piece fresh ginger, peeled and finely chopped

300 g shiitake mushrooms, stems removed and caps quartered

½ Chinese cabbage, trimmed and finely shredded

150 g bean sprouts

PANTRY

1 tablespoon vegetable oil

1 tablespoon sesame oil

1 tablespoon light soy sauce

Chinese cabbage combined with mushrooms results in an earthy, savoury stir-fry. Fresh shiitake are used here but you could use dried shiitake, pre-soaked in a bowl with boiling water for 1 hour.

—

Heat the vegetable and sesame oils in a wok over high heat. Swirl the wok around to coat in the oils. Add the ginger and mushrooms and stir-fry for 2–3 minutes, until the mushrooms are tender.

Add the cabbage and bean sprouts, then pour in the soy sauce around the edge of the wok. Stir-fry for 3 minutes until all the vegetables are golden and tender. Transfer to a serving plate and serve hot.

NOODLES & RICE
麵食和米飯

ANTS CLIMBING TREE

螞蟻上樹

SERVES: *4 TO SHARE*   **PREPARATION:** *10 MINUTES*   **COOKING:** *10 MINUTES*

FRESH

200 g minced pork

1 tablespoon finely grated fresh ginger

2 spring onions, white and green parts
  finely sliced and separated

2 quantities Chilli Sauce
  (see page 210)

PANTRY

100 g bean thread noodles

1 teaspoon dark soy sauce

2 teaspoons sesame oil

1 tablespoon vegetable oil

This recipe title is very typical of the evocative language used to describe a dish in China. The small flecks of pork clinging to the noodles are supposed to resemble ants climbing the fine branches of a tree. It really is one of the tastiest Chinese noodle dishes you could eat.

—

Put the noodles in a bowl and cover with warm water. Set aside for 5 minutes, then drain.

Combine the pork, dark soy sauce and sesame oil in a bowl. Stir until well combined.

Heat the vegetable oil in a wok or large frying pan over high heat. Swirl the wok around to coat in the oil. Add the ginger and white parts of the spring onion and stir-fry for just a few seconds.

Add the Chilli Sauce and pork mixture and stir-fry for 4–5 minutes, breaking up the meat so it is well browned and combined with the seasonings. Pour in 60 ml water and stir-fry for just a minute until thickened.

Stir the noodles through the pork mixture and transfer to a serving plate. Sprinkle over the green parts of the spring onion and serve.

SPICY BEIJING NOODLES
香辣北京拉麵

SERVES: 4   PREPARATION: 15 MINUTES   COOKING: 15 MINUTES

FRESH

2 spring onions, white and green parts
finely sliced and separated

3 cm piece fresh ginger, peeled and
finely grated

400 g minced pork

500 g thick wheat noodles

1 cucumber, finely sliced
into matchsticks

SPICES

1 teaspoon ground
Szechuan peppercorns

PANTRY

1 tablespoon vegetable oil

2 tablespoons chilli bean sauce

This recipe exemplifies the influence that Chinese cuisine has had on the world stage. Noodles were created in China and made their way around the world, ending up in Italy as pasta. No surprises to learn that this dish is also referred to as Chinese spaghetti bolognese!

—

Heat the oil in a wok over high heat. Swirl the wok around to coat in the oil. Add the white parts of the spring onion and the ginger and stir-fry for just a few seconds to flavour the oil.

Add the minced pork and stir-fry for 4–5 minutes until the pork is well browned. Add the chilli bean sauce and stir-fry for a minute until aromatic and dark.

Stir in 240 ml water, bring to the boil, then reduce the heat and simmer for 2–3 minutes until thickened. Remove from the heat and cover to keep warm.

Cook the noodles in boiling water for 2–3 minutes, or until they rise to the top and are tender. Drain and divide between 4 serving bowls.

Spoon the sauce over the noodles. Top with cucumber and the green parts of the spring onion, and sprinkle with the Szechuan pepper to taste.

SHANGHAI NOODLES

上海炒麵

SERVES: 4 *PREPARATION: 15 MINUTES* *RESTING: 10 MINUTES* *COOKING: 10 MINUTES*

FRESH

300 g pork scotch fillet, sliced into thin strips

400 g hokkein noodles

2 garlic cloves, chopped

2 spring onions, finely chopped

bunch Chinese broccoli, finely shredded

PANTRY

2 tablespoons oyster sauce

1 teaspoon sesame oil

3 tablespoons vegetable oil

Like many Chinese noodle dishes, this one uses very little meat. The noodles are the star ingredient. Thick and hearty hokkein noodles come from the south-east of China where they are a staple in many stir-fries.

—

Combine the pork in a bowl with 1 tablespoon of the oyster sauce. Set aside for 10 minutes.

Cook the noodles in boiling water for 2–3 minutes until tender. Drain well and set aside.

Heat the vegetable oil in a wok over high heat. Add the pork and fry for 2–3 minutes until golden. Use a slotted spoon to remove the pork to a plate.

Pour off all but 1 tablespoon of oil from the wok. Add the garlic, spring onions and Chinese broccoli and stir-fry for 1 minute until the greens have wilted.

Return the pork to the wok and add the remaining oyster sauce and sesame oil. Stir for a few seconds to combine then add the noodles and 3 tablespoons water. Cook until the sauce thickens and coats the noodles. Serve hot.

SESAME NOODLES WITH GARLIC CHIVES & BEAN SPROUTS

芝麻豉油王炒麵

SERVES: 4 TO SHARE   **PREPARATION:** 10 MINUTES   **COOKING:** 10 MINUTES

FRESH

400 g thin egg noodles

bunch garlic chives, cut into
  2 cm lengths

200 g bean sprouts

PANTRY

2 tablespoons vegetable oil

2 teaspoons sesame oil

1 tablespoon light soy sauce

1 teaspoon toasted sesame seeds

These noodles are a favourite at dim sum. They can be served as part of a meal and make a delicious alternative to fried rice.

—

Cook the noodles in boiling water for 2–3 minutes, stirring to separate. Rinse under cold water and drain well.

Put the noodles in a bowl with 1 tablespoon of the vegetable oil. Toss the noodles around to coat in the oil and set aside.

Heat a wok over high heat. Add the remaining vegetable oil and the sesame oil. Swirl the wok around to coat in the oil. Add the garlic chives and bean sprouts and stir-fry for just 1 minute until the vegetables are tender.

Add the noodles and stir-fry for 2–3 minutes. Add the soy sauce by pouring it around the edge of the wok. Stir-fry for 1 minute until all the ingredients are well combined. Transfer to a large serving plate and sprinkle with the sesame seeds.

TANGY SALAD WITH COLD NOODLES

濃香凉拌麵

SERVES: 4 TO SHARE   *PREPARATION: 10 MINUTES*   *COOKING: 5 MINUTES*

FRESH

small bunch coriander, leaves and
  stems roughly chopped

2 spring onions, finely sliced

PANTRY

3 tablespoons Chinese black vinegar

3 tablespoons light soy sauce

1 tablespoon sesame oil

1 teaspoon white sugar

300 g wheat noodles

This is a refreshing cold noodle salad made extra tangy by the inclusion of vinegar in the dressing. Black vinegar is made from glutinous rice and malt and is similar to balsamic vinegar.

—

Combine the vinegar, soy sauce, sesame oil and white sugar in a small bowl. Set aside.

Cook the noodles in boiling water for 2–3 minutes until tender. Rinse under cold water and drain well.

Combine the noodles in a large bowl with the dressing, coriander and spring onions. Toss to combine and transfer to a serving plate.

CHAR KWAY TEOW
(STIR-FRIED RICE CAKE STRIPS)

炒貴刁

SERVES: 4　　*PREPARATION: 20 MINUTES*　　*COOKING: 10 MINUTES*

FRESH

400 g fresh rice noodles, 1 cm thick

2 spring onions, chopped

bunch garlic chives, cut into
　2 cm lengths

12 medium raw prawns, peeled
　and deveined

2 eggs, beaten

PANTRY

1 tablespoon vegetable oil

2 Chinese sausages (*lap cheong*),
　finely sliced

2 tablespoons oyster sauce

This noodle dish is popular not only in China but most of South-east Asia. It is distinguished by using flat rice noodles and almost always includes prawns and pork sausage or barbecued pork.

—

Rinse the rice noodles under warm water and gently separate. Drain well and set aside.

Heat the oil in a wok over high heat. Swirl the wok around to coat in the oil. Add the spring onions, garlic chives and Chinese sausage and stir-fry for 2–3 minutes until the spring onions are soft and golden.

Add the prawns and stir-fry for 2 minutes until the prawns are pink and cooked through.

Add the noodles and oyster sauce and stir-fry until combined. Pour the eggs around the edges of the wok. Stir-fry for a couple of minutes, until the eggs are cooked and well combined with the noodles. Transfer to a serving plate and serve hot.

SINGAPORE NOODLES

星洲炒米

SERVES: 4 TO SHARE　　*PREPARATION: 10 MINUTES*　　*COOKING: 10 MINUTES*

FRESH

1 red onion, finely chopped

1 green capsicum (pepper), finely
 sliced

150 g raw medium prawns, peeled
 and deveined

120 g bean sprouts

Chilli Sauce (see page 210), to serve
 (optional)

SPICES

1 tablespoon curry powder

PANTRY

250 g rice vermicelli

3 tablespoons vegetable oil

2 teaspoons light soy sauce

**The dried rice noodles used here are best cooked with very little
or no sauce as they tend to absorb liquid and go soggy. Curry
powder is not often used in Chinese cooking but it is a delicious
addition to this moreish noodle dish.**

—

Put the noodles in a heatproof bowl. Cover with boiling water and
leave to soak for 3 minutes until tender. Drain well and set aside.

Heat the oil in a wok over high heat. Swirl the wok around to coat in
the oil. Add the onion and capsicum and stir-fry for 2–3 minutes until
the vegetables are tender. Add the prawns and stir-fry for 2 minutes
until pink and cooked through.

Add the curry powder and cook for just a few seconds until fragrant.
Stir through the noodles until well combined and coated in the
curry powder.

Add the soy sauce by drizzling it in around the sides of the wok. Add
the bean sprouts and stir until well combined. Transfer to a serving
plate and serve hot with Chilli Sauce on the side if liked.

STICKY RICE PARCELS

粽子

SERVES: 4   *PREPARATION: 30 MINUTES*   *SOAKING: 12 HOURS*   *COOKING: ABOUT 2¼ HOURS*

FRESH

1 boneless chicken thigh fillet, cut into
  1 cm pieces

1 spring onion, finely chopped

1 tablespoon finely grated fresh ginger

PANTRY

200 g glutinous rice

2 tablespoons small dried shrimp

5 g sliced dried shiitake mushrooms

1 tablespoon vegetable oil

1 tablespoon oyster sauce

2 teaspoons cornflour

4 dried lotus leaves or 4 large (30 cm)
  sheets baking paper

Lotus leaves are sold dried and look like a green tea–coloured fan. If lotus leaves are tricky to find, simply wrap and steam the filling in baking paper.

—

Soak the rice in cold water for 12 hours. Drain. Line a bamboo steamer basket with a clean tea towel. Add the rice, set over boiling water and steam for 1 hour. Transfer to a bowl, cover and set aside.

Meanwhile, soak both the shrimp and mushrooms in boiling water for 45 minutes until soft. Drain, chop and set aside.

Combine the oyster sauce, cornflour and 60 ml water in a small bowl.

Heat the oil in a wok over high heat. Add the chicken and stir-fry for about 2 minutes until golden. Stir in the ginger and spring onions. Add the shrimp and mushrooms and stir-fry to combine. Add the oyster sauce mixture and stir until combined. Transfer to a bowl and leave to cool.

Divide the rice into 8 equal portions. Use wet hands to smooth each ball and form into a flat disc shape.

Lay four of the rice discs on a work surface. Place equal amounts of the chicken mixture on each one. Put another rice disc on top of each. Use wet hands to press the rice together to seal the filling – it doesn't matter if some of it is sticking out.

Sit each rice ball in the centre of a lotus leaf or sheet of baking paper. Roll up to enclose, folding the edges in or twisting to seal. Sit in a bamboo steamer basket set over boiling water and steam for 1 hour. Transfer to a serving plate and unwrap at the table.

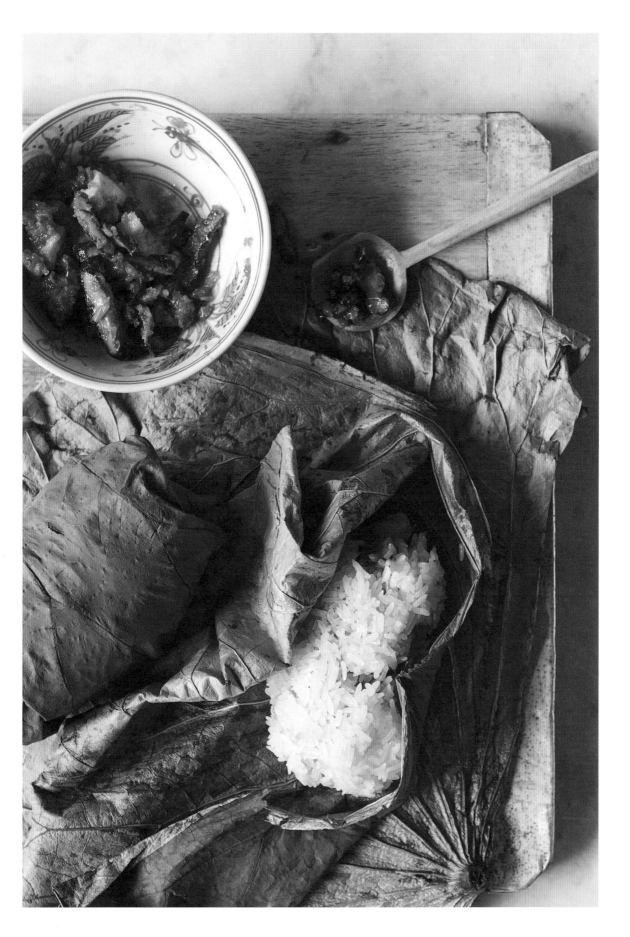

YANGZHOU FRIED RICE

揚州炒飯

SERVES: 4 TO SHARE   *PREPARATION: 20 MINUTES*   *COOKING: 10 MINUTES*

FRESH

4 eggs, beaten

3 spring onions, finely sliced

1 quantity Steamed Rice
(see page 215)

130 g frozen peas, defrosted

PANTRY

2 tablespoons vegetable oil

2 Chinese sausages (*lap cheong*),
finely sliced

1 tablespoon light soy sauce

2 teaspoons sesame oil

This is the quintessential Chinese fried rice. And what a contribution this dish has made to the world of food! Despite its worldwide fame, fried rice in China is not a fancy affair. It is what it is – quickly cooked, simply flavoured rice.

—

Heat 1 tablespoon of the oil in a wok over high heat. Swirl the wok around to coat in the oil. Pour the eggs into the wok and spread over the base. Leave for a few seconds until the eggs start to bubble and firm around the edges.

Fold the eggs from the outside to the centre and cook for 1 minute, until the eggs are just cooked through. Transfer to a chopping board and roughly chop.

Wipe the wok clean and add the remaining oil. Swirl the wok around to coat in the oil. Add the spring onions and sausage and stir-fry for about 2 minutes, until the sausage is golden.

Add the rice and peas and stir-fry for several minutes, breaking up large clumps of rice, cooking until the rice is slightly golden.

Add the soy sauce to the wok by pouring it in around the edges. Stir-fry to combine the soy sauce and transfer to a serving plate. Drizzle with the sesame oil.

VEGETARIAN FRIED RICE

揚州炒飯

SERVES: 4   PREPARATION: 15 MINUTES   COOKING: 10 MINUTES

FRESH

4 eggs

1 red onion, finely sliced into wedges

1 quantity Steamed Rice
  (see page 215)

200 g bean sprouts

small bunch coriander, leaves and
  stems finely chopped

PANTRY

2 tablespoons vegetable oil

2 teaspoons sesame oil

2 teaspoons soy sauce

This is a delicious vegetarian version of fried rice. All you need is some left-over cooked rice, a handful of fresh ingredients and just a few minutes of your time to cook a very tasty Chinese meal.

—

Beat the eggs until well combined. Heat 1 tablespoon of the oil in a wok over high heat. Swirl the wok around to coat in the oil. Add the eggs and use a spatula to push the eggs up the sides of the hot wok. Cook for 1 minute until the eggs start to set around the edges. Fold the outside of the eggs into the centre. Repeat this a few more times until the eggs are just set. Transfer the eggs to a plate.

Wipe the wok clean and add the remaining oil. Again, swirl the wok around to coat in the oil. Add the onion and stir-fry for 2–3 minutes, until golden. Add the rice and stir-fry for 2–3 minutes, breaking up larger clumps of rice. Stir in the bean sprouts and cook for a minute until tender.

Add the soy sauce and sesame oil to the wok and stir-fry until the sauces are combined with the rice. Add the eggs and coriander and stir until well combined. Transfer to a serving plate and serve.

CONGEE

粥

SERVES: 4   ***PREPARATION:*** *20 MINUTES*   ***COOKING:*** *ABOUT 1 HOUR*

FRESH

10 cm piece fresh ginger, peeled and finely sliced

1 spring onion, white and green parts finely sliced and separated

½ cooked rotisserie chicken (or Red-braised Chicken, see page 96), skin and meat shredded

PANTRY

1 litre chicken stock

100 g long-grain rice

2 tablespoons light soy sauce

2 tablespoons crispy fried shallots

Congee is slow-cooked rice that becomes silky and soft. It is also referred to as Chinese rice porridge. It is traditionally eaten with a range of tasty bits on the side: fried tofu, boiled eggs, wilted greens and pickled vegetables.

—

Combine the ginger, white parts of the spring onion, stock and 500 ml water in a large saucepan. Bring to the boil, then stir through the rice. Reduce the heat to a low simmer and cook for 1 hour until thickened and most of the liquid has been absorbed.

Stir in the chicken and soy sauce and cook for a couple of minutes until the chicken has heated through.

Serve hot with the green parts of the spring onion and crispy fried shallots scattered on top.

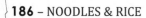

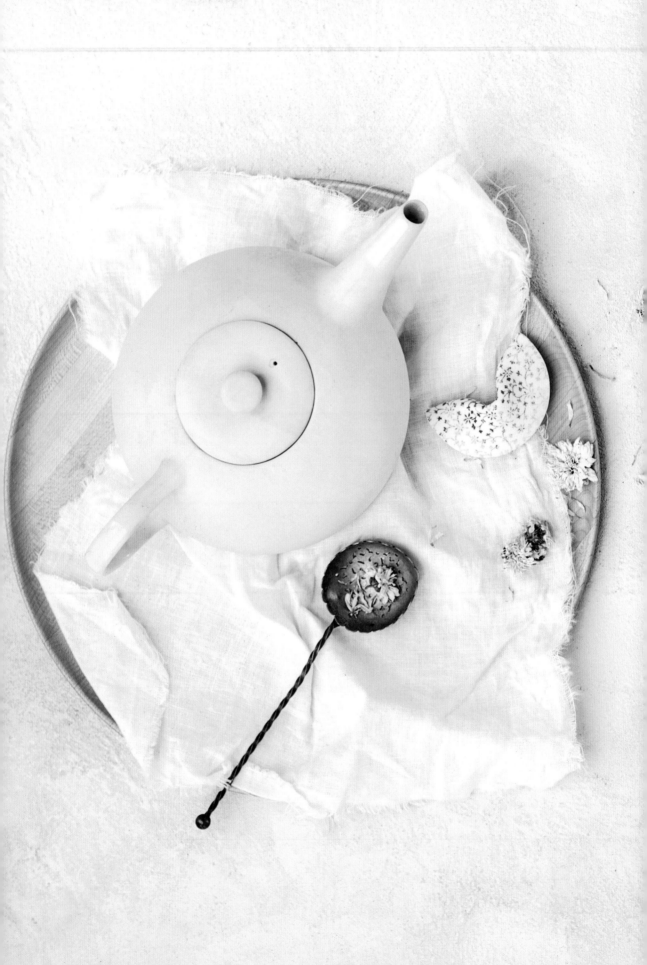

SWEETS

第七章

CANDIED WALNUTS

琥珀核桃

SERVES: 8 TO SHARE　*PREPARATION: 10 MINUTES*　*COOKING: 4–6 MINUTES*

FRESH

200 g walnut halves

SPICES

1 cinnamon stick

PANTRY

80 g white sugar

1 tablespoon honey

1 teaspoon vanilla extract

1 tablespoon toasted sesame seeds

This is a delightful sweet to have on hand. It can be simply served with Chinese tea but as a special treat, scatter the candied walnuts over a bowl of vanilla ice cream.

—

Line a baking tray with baking paper.

Combine the sugar, honey, cinnamon, vanilla and 60 ml water in a frying pan over medium heat. Cook for 2–3 minutes until the mixture boils and the sugar dissolves.

Add the walnuts and cook for 2–3 minutes, without stirring, but shaking the pan from time to time so the sugar syrup coats the walnuts.

When the sugar syrup begins to turn golden and is starting to smoke, tip the mixture onto the prepared tray. Use a fork to spread the walnuts in a single layer on the tray and sprinkle with sesame seeds.

Leave to cool completely, then transfer to an airtight container. Roughly break up to serve.

FRIED PASTRIES WITH DATE & ORANGE

香橙棗糕

MAKES: 24   *PREPARATION: 20 MINUTES*   *COOKING: 20–25 MINUTES*

FRESH

1 teaspoon finely grated orange zest

1 tablespoon orange juice

PANTRY

160 g dried dates, pitted and finely chopped

2 teaspoons light brown sugar

24 square egg wonton wrappers

vegetable oil, for frying

1 tablespoon icing sugar

These sweet little triangles, filled with date and a hint of orange, require very little effort. They can be made and frozen in advance.

—

Combine the dates, sugar, orange zest and juice in a food processor and blend to make a paste.

Put 1 teaspoon of the date mixture in the centre of a wonton wrapper. Wet the edges with water and fold over to make a triangle. Firmly press around the edges to seal. Repeat to make 24.

To cook the pastries, pour enough oil in a small saucepan to come halfway up the sides. Set over medium–high heat. The oil is ready when a wonton wrapper sizzles on contact with the oil and turns golden in 20 seconds.

Cook 2–3 pastries at a time for 2 minutes until golden. Transfer to a plate lined with paper towels. Repeat to cook all the pastries.

Finely sift the icing sugar over the pastries before serving.

ALMOND LAKE
(ALMOND MILK PUDDING)

杏仁布丁

SERVES: 8   *PREPARATION:* 15 MINUTES   *CHILLING:* 6 HOURS   *COOKING:* 10 MINUTES

FRESH

720 ml milk

175 g strawberries, chopped

pulp from 2 passionfruit

PANTRY

6 gelatine sheets

110 g white sugar

2 teaspoons almond extract

210 g tinned drained lychees

Almond lake pudding is sometimes cut into cubes or triangles to serve. This is a slightly creamier version, using less gelatine and served in individual glasses where it really does resemble an almond lake!

—

Put the gelatine sheets in a bowl and cover with cold water. Leave for 7–8 minutes until the gelatine is very soft. Drain the sheets well and set aside.

Combine the milk and sugar in a small saucepan over medium heat. Cook for a few minutes until the milk is just warm to the touch. Stir through 1 sheet of gelatine at a time until it has dissolved in the warm milk. Repeat until all the gelatine has been incorporated into the milk. Stir in the almond extract.

Pour into 8 individual serving glasses. Refrigerate for 6 hours or overnight, until firm but still a bit wobbly.

Arrange the fruit in a bowl and serve on the side to spoon over the puddings.

How to:
MAKE CHINESE TEA
如何泡中式茶

Chinese tea is a fragrant and refreshing hot beverage enjoyed any time of day. It is especially popular at *yum cha*, a meal where dumplings or small plates of food are served with tea.

EQUIPMENT

Chinese teapot

Chinese teacups

1

Arrange Chinese teacups, a Chinese teapot and a bowl of Chinese tea leaves on a tray.

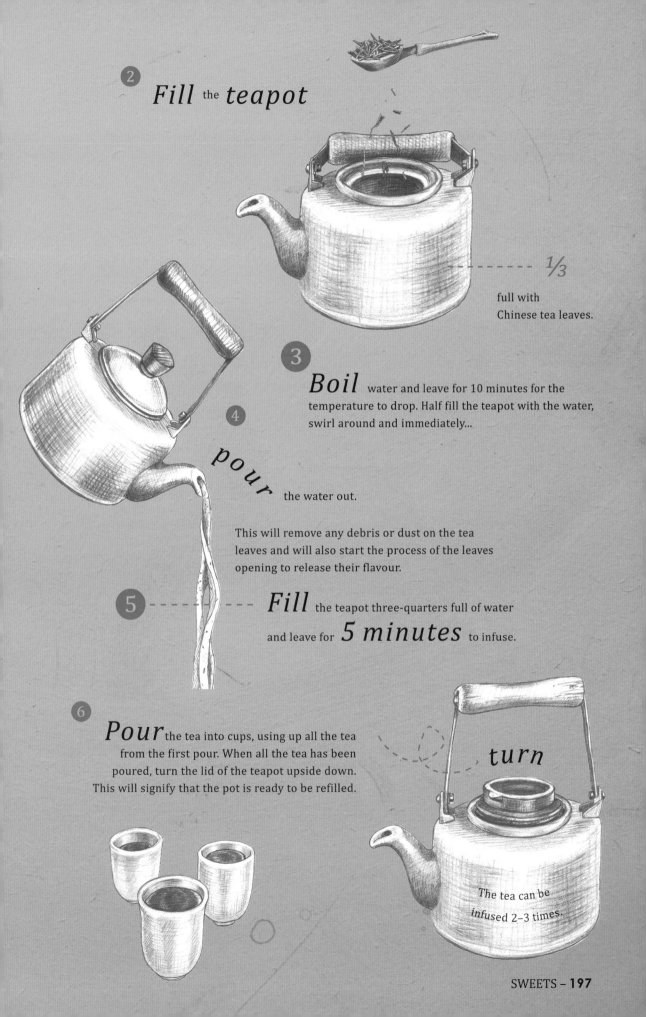

2 *Fill* the *teapot*

1/3

full with
Chinese tea leaves.

3 **Boil** water and leave for 10 minutes for the
temperature to drop. Half fill the teapot with the water,
swirl around and immediately...

4 *pour* the water out.

This will remove any debris or dust on the tea
leaves and will also start the process of the leaves
opening to release their flavour.

5 *Fill* the teapot three-quarters full of water
and leave for **5 minutes** to infuse.

6 *Pour* the tea into cups, using up all the tea
from the first pour. When all the tea has been
poured, turn the lid of the teapot upside down.
This will signify that the pot is ready to be refilled.

turn

The tea can be
infused 2–3 times.

WATERMELON SHELL
WITH FRESH FRUITS

西瓜果盤

SERVES: 6 PREPARATION: 15 MINUTES

FRESH

½ small seedless watermelon, chilled

2 mandarins, segmented

225 g cherries

1 apple, sliced into thin wedges

PANTRY

400 g tin lychees in syrup

Fresh fruit is often served after a meal in Chinese restaurants.

—

Scoop out the flesh in big pieces from the watermelon, leaving the shell intact. Chop the flesh into different shapes: squares, triangles or use a melon baller to make watermelon spheres. Put into a bowl.

Drain the lychees and reserve one-quarter of the lychee syrup.

Combine the lychees, mandarin, cherries and apple in the bowl with the watermelon. Pour over the reserved syrup and gently toss to combine.

Spoon the fruit salad back into the watermelon shell, ready to serve in small bowls.

CUSTARD TARTS

蛋撻

MAKES: 12   *PREPARATION:* 15 MINUTES   *COOKING:* 25 MINUTES

FRESH

1 x 24 cm square sheet frozen
puff pastry

butter, for greasing

1 egg, plus 1 egg yolk

80 ml milk

PANTRY

plain flour, for dusting

60 g caster sugar

Wherever you find an enclave of Chinese food stores you are bound to come across a bakery that sells these sweet little custard tarts. They are also served at *yum cha* (or dim sum) as a sweet treat.

—

Remove the pastry from the freezer to defrost. Preheat the oven to 220°C/Gas 7 and grease a 12-hole cupcake tin.

Fold the pastry in half, then firmly roll it into a log. Cut it into 12 equal-sized portions. Roll each portion on a lightly floured surface into a 12 cm circle. Cut with a 10 cm crimped cookie cutter. Press the pastries into the tin and set aside.

Combine the sugar and 100 ml water in a small saucepan. Cook over medium heat until the sugar has dissolved, then set aside.

Beat the egg and egg yolk in a small bowl until well combined. Stir in the milk and the sugar syrup. Strain the mixture into a pouring jug, then pour the custard into the pastries.

Bake for 10 minutes until the pastry is starting to puff up around the edges. Reduce the temperature to 180°C/Gas 4 and cook for 10 minutes until the custard has set and the pastry is puffed and golden. Leave to cool for 5 minutes before removing. Serve warm with tea.

ALMOND COOKIES

杏仁酥

MAKES: 24   PREPARATION: 10 MINUTES   COOKING: 20 MINUTES

FRESH

115 g butter, melted

1 egg, beaten with 1 tablespoon
   cold water

PANTRY

115 g plain flour, plus extra for dusting

½ teaspoon baking powder

110 g caster sugar

24 blanched almonds

2 tablespoons milk

The dough mixture for these cookies can be made a day or two in advance and kept in the fridge. For an extra almond flavour, try adding a drop or two of almond essence.

—

Preheat the oven to 180°C/Gas 4 and line a baking tray with baking paper.

Combine the flour, baking powder and sugar in a food processor and process for a few seconds.

With the motor running, add the butter, then the egg mixture and process for a few seconds until the mixture is well combined but still crumbly.

Tip the mixture onto a lightly floured surface and roughly knead together. The mixture won't be entirely smooth.

Roll teaspoons of the mixture between the palms of your hands to form into balls and place on the baking tray. Leave some space between each ball as they will expand when cooked. Use a broad knife to flatten each ball into a disc.

Press an almond into the centre of each cookie and brush with the milk. Bake in the oven for 18–20 minutes until golden. Transfer the cookies to a wire rack to cool. Serve with jasmine tea.

MANGO PANCAKES

芒果班戟

SERVES: 4   *PREPARATION: 20 MINUTES*   *CHILLING: 1 HOUR*   *COOKING: 10 MINUTES*

FRESH

2 eggs

165 ml milk

1 tablespoon butter, melted, plus extra
  for greasing

120 ml thin (pouring) cream

1 ripe mango, finely diced (or 185 g
  tinned mango, drained and diced)

PANTRY

75 g plain flour

3 tablespoons icing sugar

yellow food colouring (optional)

These delicious pancakes filled with freshly whipped cream and mangoes are a favourite sweet treat for dim sum. They are easily made at home and the mango can be replaced with strawberries, lychees or banana.

—

Combine the eggs and milk in a bowl, whisking until well combined.

Whisk in the butter, flour and 2 tablespoons of the icing sugar until smooth and well combined. If using the yellow food colouring, stir in a few drops to achieve the desired colour. Refrigerate for at least 1 hour for the batter to thicken.

Beat the cream and remaining 1 tablespoon icing sugar until the mixture is very thick. Refrigerate until needed.

To cook the pancakes, lightly grease a large non-stick frying pan. Heat over medium heat and add 3 tablespoons of the batter to the pan, swirling the pan around so the batter forms a 20 cm circle.

Cook for 2 minutes, so the pancake sets but doesn't brown. Transfer to a plate. Repeat to make 4 pancakes. Leave to cool. These can be made several hours in advance.

Stir the mango through the cream. To assemble the pancakes, place a pancake on a clean work surface. Put one-quarter of the mango cream in the centre of the pancake. Fold the edge nearest you over the filling. Fold in the sides, then roll into a log shape. Repeat to make 4 pancakes.

MANDARIN
TAPIOCA PUDDING

柑橘西米露

SERVES: 6   **PREPARATION:** 30 MINUTES   **CHILLING:** 6 HOURS   **COOKING:** 15 MINUTES

FRESH

120 ml milk

80 ml thin (pouring) cream

PANTRY

70 g tapioca pearls

400 g tin of mandarin segments
   in syrup

80 g caster sugar

Tapioca pearls are an old-fashioned ingredient. Preparing them requires very little effort and results in a very comforting pudding.

—

Cook the tapioca in a saucepan of boiling water for 10 minutes. Remove from the heat, cover and leave for 20 minutes, until the tapioca pearls are translucent. Rinse under cold water and drain very well. Set aside.

Drain the mandarin segments and reserve 2 tablespoons of the syrup from the tin. Set aside.

Combine the milk, cream and sugar in a small saucepan. Cook over medium heat for about 5 minutes, stirring until the sugar has dissolved. Remove from the heat and stir in the tapioca until well combined.

Stir the mandarin syrup and half the mandarin segments into the pudding mixture. Spoon into 6 serving glasses and refrigerate for about 6 hours. Serve with the remaining mandarin segments on top of each pudding.

BASICS

餅乾

CHILLI SAUCE

辣椒醬

MAKES: 500 ML
PREPARATION: 5 MINUTES
COOKING: 5 MINUTES

FRESH

24 large red chillies, ends trimmed and
  roughly chopped (about 200 g)

6 garlic cloves, chopped

10 cm piece fresh ginger, peeled
  and chopped

PANTRY

120 ml vegetable oil

2 tablespoons light brown sugar

3 tablespoons light soy sauce

**This chilli sauce is made with fresh
chillies. It's delicious and addictive and
goes with just about any dish.**

—

Put the fresh chillies, garlic and ginger in
a food processor and process to a finely
chopped paste.

Heat the oil in a wok over medium–high heat.
Add the chilli paste and stir-fry for 3 minutes
until softened and aromatic.

Stir in the brown sugar and cook for 1 minute
until the sugar has completely dissolved
in the paste. Add the soy sauce. Cook for
1 minute, then remove from the heat.

Leave to cool, then transfer to a clean glass
jar. This sauce can be eaten straight away or
kept covered in the fridge for up to 1 week.

GINGER & SPRING ONION SAUCE

薑葱醬

MAKES: 125 ML
PREPARATION: 5 MINUTES
COOKING: 2 MINUTES

FRESH

100 g finely sliced spring onions

20 g fresh ginger, peeled and cut into
  thin matchsticks

PANTRY

3 tablespoons vegetable oil

1 tablespoon sesame oil

½ teaspoon caster sugar

1 teaspoon light soy sauce

**This is a great recipe to have in your
repertoire. It uses the very Chinese
technique of pouring hot oil onto the
spring onions and ginger.**

—

Combine the spring onions and ginger in
a heatproof bowl.

Combine the vegetable and sesame oils in a
small saucepan. Cook over high heat. When
the oil mixture is smoking hot, carefully
pour it over the spring onions and ginger,
causing them to sizzle.

Stir to combine then add the sugar and
soy sauce. Cover and store in the fridge
for 2–3 days.

CHILLI SALT

辣椒鹽

This spicy salt keeps for ages. It is great to have this on hand to sprinkle over just about anything, but it goes especially well with fried and grilled meats, seafood and chicken.

MAKES: 4 TEASPOONS   *PREPARATION:* 5 MINUTES

SPICES

1 teaspoon chilli powder

1 teaspoon white pepper

2 teaspoons sea salt

Combine all the ingredients and store in an airtight container.

FIVE-SPICE

五香粉

Five-spice is the quintessential Chinese spice mix. It is used to deeply flavour slow-braised and roasted meats and chicken. To make more, simply double or triple the quantity. It will keep for ages, stored in an airtight container.

MAKES: 50 G
PREPARATION: 5 MINUTES

SPICES

2 cinnamon sticks

3 star anise

1 teaspoon Szechuan peppercorns

½ teaspoon fennel seeds

2 cloves

Combine all the ingredients and store in an airtight container.

FIVE-SPICE SALT

五香鹽

The spices in the five-spice mixture can be ground down to make an aromatic powder. Combined with sea salt, this is a delicious addition to fried foods and salads.

MAKES: 75 G
PREPARATION: 5 MINUTES

SPICES

1 quantity of Five-spice (see above)

1 tablespoon sea salt flakes

Put the Five-spice in a spice grinder or coffee mill and blend to a powder. Transfer to a small bowl and stir in the salt. Store in an airtight container.

SZECHUAN DIPPING SAUCE

四川蘸醬

Chilli oil is a fiery red oil that is used in abundance in Szechuan cooking. Here, a small amount is added to the sauce to give real bite. This sauce is great with dumplings, seafood and chicken.

MAKES: 125 ML
PREPARATION: 2 MINUTES

PANTRY

3 tablespoons Chinese black vinegar

2 tablespoons light soy sauce

1 tablespoon sesame oil

1 teaspoon chilli oil

½ teaspoon caster sugar

Combine the ingredients in a bowl, stirring until the sugar has dissolved. Cover and refrigerate for 2–3 days.

CHILLI & SOY SAUCE

醬油拌辣椒

Small fresh red chillies are used here. They can be super hot, so remove the seeds if you want to reduce the heat but keep all the flavour.

MAKES: 125 ML
PREPARATION: 2 MINUTES

FRESH

2 small red chillies, finely sliced

2 garlic cloves, finely chopped

1 spring onion, finely chopped

PANTRY

3 tablespoons light soy sauce

½ teaspoon caster sugar

Combine the ingredients in a bowl, stirring until the sugar has dissolved. Cover and refrigerate for 2–3 days.

STEAMED RICE

蒸米飯

A bowl of hot steamed rice may well be the essence of Chinese food. Many of us are familiar with boiled rice and this is a perfectly acceptable way to cook rice. Steaming rice is how rice is cooked in an electric rice cooker. But you don't need a rice cooker to make it – just a saucepan and some cold water!

MAKES: *740 G*　　***PREPARATION:*** *5 MINUTES*　　***COOKING:*** *15 MINUTES*

PANTRY

300 g jasmine rice

Wash the rice in several changes of cold water until the water is clear. Transfer the rice to a medium saucepan and add 750 ml water. Cook over high heat until the water boils rapidly and forms steaming holes.

Reduce the heat to low, cover the pan with a tightly fitting lid and cook for 12 minutes, without removing the lid. Remove from the heat and quickly fluff the rice with a fork. Cover for a further 5 minutes.

MANDARIN (PEKING) PANCAKES

北京春餅

MAKES: 24   PREPARATION: 10 MINUTES   RESTING: 30 MINUTES
COOKING: 10 MINUTES

PANTRY

300 g plain flour, plus extra for dusting

1–2 tablespoons sesame oil

Ready-made Peking pancakes are sold in some Asian food stores but they are very easy to make at home. Two pancakes sandwich a thin layer of sesame oil. When gently pan-fried, the pancakes are golden on one side and softly steamed on the other. The perfect savoury pancake!

—

Put the flour in a food processor. With the motor running, add 180 ml boiling water, plus a little extra if needed, until it forms into a ball.

Tip the dough onto a lightly floured work surface and briefly knead to form a smooth ball. Cover with a clean cloth and set aside for 30 minutes.

Cut the dough in half. Lightly flour a work surface and roll one portion of dough until it is 2–3 mm thick. Cut out circles using a 7 cm round cutter to make at least 12 circles. Repeat with the other portion of the dough to make 24 circles in total.

Lightly brush one side of half the circles with sesame oil and put another one on top, gently pressing them together to seal. Roll these circles on a lightly floured surface until they are about 15 cm across and very thin.

Heat a large non-stick frying pan over medium–high heat. Working in batches, cook the pancakes for about 1 minute each side until golden and steam puffs out from the centre. Transfer to a plate and cover to keep warm.

These can be made a day in advance and kept covered in the fridge. To reheat, wrap in foil and cook in a 180°C/Gas 4 oven for 10 minutes.

DUMPLING DOUGH

餃子麵糰

MAKES: 12   *PREPARATION: 10 MINUTES*   *RESTING: 30 MINUTES*

PANTRY

190 g plain flour, plus extra for
  dusting

The best dumplings you can eat will be made using handmade dumpling dough. These are slightly thicker than ready-made wrappers. The silky dough forms the perfect parcel in which to enclose a delicious filling that can be boiled, pan-fried or steamed.

—

Put the flour in a food processor. With the motor running, slowly add 180 ml cold water and process until the mixture forms into a ball. Add 1–2 extra tablespoons water if needed for the dough to come together.

Tip the dough onto a lightly floured work surface and knead for a couple of minutes to form a smooth ball of dough. Wrap in plastic wrap and set aside for 30 minutes.

Gently knead the dough on a lightly floured work surface and cut into 3 equal portions. Working with one portion at a time, roll the dough so it is very thin. Cut out circles using an 8 cm cutter.

Lightly dust each one with flour and transfer to a plate. Cover with plastic wrap until needed. These can be made a day in advance if kept in the fridge.

MEAL PLANNER

菜單

There is a menu here for just about any occasion and any time of day! This exemplifies the versatility of Chinese food. Many of the dishes suit dietary requirements, such as gluten-free, and the cuisine also offers so many choices for vegans and vegetarians.

YUM CHA: Siu Mai (see page 30), Prawn Spring Rolls (see page 36), Bean Curd Spring Rolls (see page 38), Char Siu (see page 114), Custard Tarts (see page 200).

LUNCH: Yangzhou Fried Rice (see page 182), Crispy Chicken with Ginger & Spring Onion Sauce (see page 98), Stir-fried Beef & Capsicum with Black Bean Sauce (see page 128), Stir-fried Chinese Cabbage (see page 162), Mango Pancakes (see page 204).

MIDWEEK DINNER: Tangy Salad with Cold Noodles (see page 174), Steamed Rice (see page 215), Stir-fried Asparagus, Baby Corn & Snow Peas (see page 160), Three-cup Chicken (see page 82), Mandarin Tapioca Pudding (see page 206).

VEGAN DINNER: Hot & Sour Soup (see page 46), Fried Tofu with Spiced Salt (see page 142), Tomato & Black Fungus with Tangy Glass Noodles (see page 144), Buddha's Delight (see page 154), Watermelon Shell with Fresh Fruits (see page 198).

SEAFOOD SPECIAL: Steamed Prawn & Rice Noodle Rolls (see page 32), Salt & Pepper Squid (see page 60), Stir-fried Mussels with Black Bean & Chilli (see page 64), Seafood Hotpot with Vermicelli Noodles (see page 66), Almond Cookies (see page 202).

CASUAL STREET FOOD: Spring Onion Pancakes (see page 24), Siu Mai (see page 30), Ma Po Tofu (see page 120), Spicy Beijing Noodles (see page 168), Candied Walnuts (see page 190).

CHINESE NEW YEAR BANQUET: Pork & Cabbage Spring Rolls (see page 34), Sesame Noodles with Garlic Chives (see page 172), Dumplings Two Ways (see page 40), Steamed Whole Fish (see page 62), Fried Pastries with Date & Orange (see page 192).

INDEX

To my dad, Ronnie. Forever loved and thanked
for passing on his love of good food and cooking.

Published in 2020 by Murdoch Books,
an imprint of Allen & Unwin
First published in 2019 by Hachette Livre (Marabout)

Murdoch Books Australia
83 Alexander Street
Crows Nest NSW 2065
Phone: +61 (0) 2 8425 0100
murdochbooks.com.au
info@murdochbooks.com.au

Murdoch Books UK
Ormond House, 26–27 Boswell Street
London WC1N 3JZ
Phone: +44 (0) 20 8785 5995
murdochbooks.co.uk
info@murdochbooks.co.uk

For corporate orders & custom publishing,
contact our business development team at
salesenquiries@murdochbooks.com.au

Publisher: Corinne Roberts
English-language editor: Shan Wolody
Photographer: Lisa Linder
Internal design & illustration: Alice Chadwick
Cover design: Estee Sarsfield
Food and prop stylist: Frankie Unsworth
Production director: Lou Playfair

Text © 2019 Marabout
The moral rights of the author have been asserted.

ISBN 978 1 76052 551 4 Australia
ISBN 978 1 91163 271 9 UK

A catalogue record for this book
is available from the National
Library of Australia

A catalogue record for this book is available
from the British Library
Printed and bound in China by Hang Tai Printing Company
Limited.

Acknowledgements

A very big thank you to the team involved in
the production of this book. It's been very
much a global effort. I'm very appreciative of
the opportunity given to me by Catie Ziller,
publisher. Thank you Abi Waters for rounding
up all the loose ends with the editing. The
delightfully whimsical illustrations are by Alice
Chadwick. These unique illustrations and her
keen design skills really make this one very
special book. And one could not ask for a more
professional and gorgeous studio team. Lisa
Linder, photographer, and Frankie Unsworth,
stylist – it was a pleasure from beginning to end.
Thanks :)

Ross Dobson grew up in the suburbs of Sydney,
Australia. His neighbours had moved to Australia
from all over the world. But it was the food of his
childhood friend, Simon Chung, that enthralled
Ross the most. This family from Hong Kong
shared their food and recipes with Ross and
his family. It was no surprise that Ross did his
first cooking course in Chinese food when he
was fourteen.

Ross is a successful author of many cookbooks.
His first book, *Chinatown*, explores the flavours
of Chinese ingredients. His other bestselling titles
include *Fired Up*, *King of the Grill*, *Food Plus Beer*
and *The Food of Argentina*.

Ross has owned and operated a café at an art
gallery, a tapas restaurant and a pop-up Chinese
yum cha-style eatery. When he isn't creating and
testing recipes from home, he is pursuing his
other great loves – travel and cooking Asian food.